Miss Charming's Book of

crazy cocktails

Also by Cheryl Charming

Miss Charming's Book of Bar Amusements: 80 Tricks

Guaranteed to Entertain Your Friends,

Break the Ice at a Bar, and Liven Up Your Next Party!

Miss Charming's Book of

crazy cocktails

Over 200 Outrageous
Drink Recipes
to Turn Any Night
Into a Party

CHERYL CHARMING

THREE RIVERS PRESS
NEW YORK

Published by Three Rivers Press, New York, New York.
Member of the Crown Publishing Group,
a division of Random House, Inc.

www.randomhouse.com

THREE RIVERS PRESS and the Tugboat design are registered
trademarks of Random House, Inc.

Printed in the United States of America

Design by Kay Schuckhart/Blond on Pond

Library of Congress Cataloging-in-Publication Data is available
under control number 2002002301.

ISBN 0-609-80914-8

10 9 8 7 6 5 4 3 2 1

First Edition

To all the crazy and wonderful people
who have shared their recipes with me
throughout the twenty-two years that I have tended bar;
to Carrie Thornton, Sarah Silbert, and Tim Roethgen
for their talent and direction;
and of course, most important, to the Source,
which resides inside me.

Thank-Yous

Thanks to Connie, John, and Barry Butcher for their mature and creative feedback. To the many UF students for letting me pick their ripe college brains. And to Dewana, Janis, and Heather for being so nice.

Contents

Miss Charming's Lingo, Barware, Mixers, Measures, and Flavor Guide

Before you read another word, walk your pretty little fingers up to the corner of this page and bend it down. Go ahead. I'll wait. . . . You now have this reference page marked for your convenience. Trust me, cocktail lover, you'll need to turn back to this page a few times because the lingo in this crazy cocktail book is a little different from that used in traditional books of mixology. If you just can't wait to get to the good stuff, then go ahead and read your eyeballs out, party animal, but you'll be back. Maybe not today, maybe not tomorrow, but soon, and for the rest of your life.

Lingo

Blend = Using the electric blender, baby. Push those buttons!

Cupa = Cup = 8 ounces.

Dasha = Dash = Just a little bit.

Float = Gently pour on top of a drink.

Garnish = Edible drink decoration.

Jig = Jigger = 1½ ounces.

Layer = Gently pouring lighter liquors on top of heavier ones to create layers. Dude, use a spoon or maraschino cherry to break the fall of the liquor.

Muddle = To crush up ingredients with a muddler.

On the rocks = Over ice.

Ounce = Duh.

Pony = 1 ounce.

Rim = To put something on the rim of the glass.

Shake = Shake, shake it up in a shaker tin, baby.

Splasha = Splash = Just a little bit more than its cousin the Dasha.

Spoona = Spoon = Duh, like a spoonful, dude.

Strain = Straining the drink with a strainer to keep the ice from coming out of the shaker tin.

Toddy = Hot H_2O drink usually made with lemon and honey, but can also just mean a hot drink.

Twist = Thin piece of a lemon rind that you twist to release the citrus oils. You then rim the glass with the oils and drop it in the drink.

BarWare

Jigger = That little two-sided metal measuring utensil.

Muddler = Short, thick wooden stick that's used to crush ingredients (used mainly for Mint Juleps and Old-Fashioneds).

Shaker tin = Stainless-steel shaker used to shake up drinks.

Strainer = A sievelike device that is placed on top of a shaker tin to keep the ice from coming out of it.

Glassware

Highball glass = 7–9 ounces

Hurricane glass = 12+ ounces (Tall, curvy tropical glass.)

Martini glass = 5 ounces (Used for martinis and shooters. Also called a cocktail glass.)

Pint glass = 16 ounces (Usually for beer, but can be used as an all-purpose tall cool glass.)

Pony glass = 1 ounce (Little stemmed curvy glass.)

Rocks glass = 5–7 ounces (Little brother of the highball glass.)

Tall cool glass = 12+ ounces

Shooter glass = 5 ounces (A rocks glass or a martini glass works well.)

Shot glass = 1½ ounces

Snifter = Can be found in various sizes; 6 ounce, 12 ounce, and 24 ounce are the most popular. Here's a really cool way to pour a perfect serving in a snifter: Lay the glass on its side with one hand and pour in the alcohol with the other hand. When the alcohol reaches the rim of the glass, you've poured a perfect serving.

Wineglass = An all-purpose wineglass is 12 ounces. A glass for white wine is 8–9 ounces, and one for red is between 13–14 ounces. A proper serving of wine is between

5–6 ounces. Keep in mind that there should be a lot of breathing room left in the wineglass when pouring a proper serving.

Marvelous Mixers

Bitters = Bittersweet liquid flavored with herbs, barks, roots, and plants. Can be found in the mixer section of your local grocery store.

Cream = Heavy cream/half-and-half/milk/soy milk/whatever your diet allows you to use.

Cream of coconut = Thick, sweet, and yummy coconut cream that can be found in cans in the mixer section of your local grocery store.

Ginger beer = Nonalcoholic beverage found in the soda section of your local grocery store.

Grenadine = Thick cherry syrup.

Lemonade = Lemon juice, H_2O, and sugar, or just use the powdered mix.

Limeade = Lime-flavored mix that comes in cans of frozen concentrate.

Lime juice = Lime "syrup" that can be found in the mixer section (not fresh-squeezed lime juice).

Pop Rocks = Candy that pops when put in your mouth.

Sweet-n-sour = This is probably the most confusing mixer of all. Not anymore! Basically it's sweet water with lime flavoring. You'll see it in the stores in the mixer section, labeled as "sour mix," "margarita mix," or "sweet-n-sour mix." Without a doubt, the very best sweet-n-sour is the kind that you make yourself. Make homemade sweet-n-sour by shaking up one cup of sugar with two cups of warm water then squeeze in some fresh lime juice. Your goal is to reach a perfect balance of sweet and a perfect balance of sour. Remember those sweet-n-sour suckers you loved as a kid? Like that. You can store it in the fridge for a few days because the cold and the sugar serve as great preservatives.

Sugar water = Water and sugar mixed together.

Whipped cream = Get the cans, baby.

Worcestershire = You'll find it near the steak sauces at your local grocery store.

Fantabulous Alcohol Flavor chart

Amaretto = Almond

Anisette (AN-ih-seht) = Licorice

Applejack = Apple

Aquavit = Strong Scandinavian liquor flavored with caraway seed

Blue curaçao (KYOOR-uh-soh) = Orange

Boone's Farm Wine = Inexpensive brand of wine that be found in any convenience store

Cassis (kah-SEES) = Black currant

Chambord = Raspberry

Coffee liqueur = Chocolate coffee

Cointreau (KWAHN-troh) = Orange

Crème de cacao (krehm deuh kah-KAY-oh) = Chocolate

Crème de menthe (white and green) = Mint

Crème de noyaux (krehm deuh nwah-YOH) = Almond

De Kuyper Sour Apple Pucker Schnapps = Sour apple

Drambuie (dram-BOO-ee) = Honey, scotch whiskey, herbs

Dry vermouth (ver-MOOTH) = White wine fortified with herbs and spices

Frangelico = Hazelnut

Galliano = Licorice, vanilla

Goldschlager = Cinnamon

Grand Marnier (GRAN mahr-NYAY) = Orange cognac

Guinness = Dark Irish beer (stout)

Irish cream = Irish whiskey, cream

Jägermeister (YAH-ger-mice-ter) = Herbs, spices

Licor 43 = Sweet citrus-vanilla

Malibu = Coconut rum

MD 20/20 (Mad Dog 20/20) = Inexpensive brand of wine that can be found in any convenience store

Ouzo (OO-zoh) = Licorice

Pimm's No. 1 = Citrus spice

Port = Sweet wine fortified with herbs and spices

Rumple Minze = Peppermint

Sambuca (sam-BOO-kuh) = Licorice

Sloe gin = Sloeberry

Southern Comfort = Peach, honey, bourbon

Sweet vermouth (ver-MOOTH) = Red wine

fortified with herbs and spices and colored with caramel

Tequila Rose = Strawberry tequila

Tia Maria = Rum coffee

Triple sec = Orange

Tuaca (tah-WAH-ka) = Vanilla, caramel brandy, orange

Yukon Jack = Canadian honey whiskey

Introduction

The first drink I ever made was at a popular little nightclub in Little Rock, Arkansas, called The Cabaret. The drink was a Piña Colada. The second drink I made was a Piña Colada, and, as a matter of fact, the third and fourth drink I made happened to be Piña Coladas, too, because the hit cocktail song "Escape (The Piña Colada Song)," by Rupert Holmes, was being played constantly over the airwaves. I'm sure that all around the world, bartenders like me were burning out countless blenders, fingering more maraschino cherries than a soda jerk, coming up with creative comebacks to "Do you like getting caught in the rain or making love at midnight?," and wanting to find this Rupert Holmes guy and strangle him. It was during this time that I made up my first drink, which was called the Nada Colada (Not a Colada). A phrase my fellow bartenders and I would say when someone ordered a Piña Colada.

After my Piña Colada initiation into the bartender world, I escaped with my cherry-stained fingers to the Caribbean and tended bar on a cruise ship. I guess I was so excited to get out of Arkansas that it didn't even dawn on me that I had headed straight for Piña Colada Land, where I made about 1,001 more Piña Coladas. It was out on the ocean blue that I started to get creative with the Coladas by adding all kinds of yummy liqueurs and flavors to the mix and giving them all kinds of fun and crazy names. From there I went to work at Walt Disney World, opening up Pleasure Island, then over to the Grand Floridian Beach Resort and Spa where, without a doubt, you will find the best Piña Coladas in all of Walt Disney World.

I didn't just stop at Piña Coladas, folks—over the years I would take ordinary, standard drink recipes, jazz them up, give them crazy names, draw them on my trusty three-by-five-inch index cards with colorful markers, and insert them into little photo albums. People loved the cards—and the recipes, too.

Most of the recipes in this book are from those homemade drink books and also from the crazy and wonderful people who have shared their drinks with me over the years and allowed me to tweak them. They are meant to be a part of joyful celebrations and good times with friends and family. Don't feel left out if you are under the legal drinking age, pregnant, or just don't like the taste of alcohol. You can make them non-alcoholic by simply leaving out the booze. Also, if you have a half-a-brain Colada head, don't drink and drive because, remember . . . life is good.

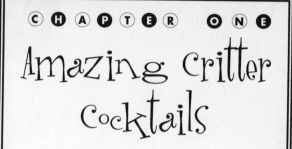

Ⓒ Ⓗ Ⓐ Ⓟ Ⓣ Ⓔ Ⓡ   Ⓞ Ⓝ Ⓔ

Amazing Critter Cocktails

Animal Cocktails More Fun Than a Barrel of Monkeys

Hey, party animal! Are you dog tired of looking for cocktails that are more fun than a barrel of monkeys? Well then, Amazing Critter Cocktails are the cat's meow, caged with wild and tame concoctions that will make you howl at the moon or bring out the beast in you. Remember, if you plan to drink like a fish and get drunk as a skunk, don't throw a monkey wrench in and get behind the wheel of a car. It's a jungle out there!

JIG THE DARK RUM
HALF JIG THE AMARETTO
FILL WITH COLA
TALL COOL GLASS

Lounge Lizard

If you are one swinging hip cat who loves the nightlife and loves to boogie, then slither up to the bar and order this tall cool concoction. Tell the bartender to find a tall cool glass of ice then add the dark rum, amaretto, and cola. It tastes so good that soon you'll be saying, "Iguana another one!"

● ● ● ● ● ● ● ● ● ● ● ● ● ● ● ● ● ●

Chocolate-covered Grasshopper

PONY THE WHITE CRÈME
DE CACAO
JIG THE GREEN CRÈME
DE MENTHE
TRIPLE JIG THE CREAM
TALL COOL GLASS OR MUG

Jiminy Cricket! Bounce all the ingredients in a shaker with ice and jump all over the joint. Strain into a fancy glass, rub your legs together, and let your conscience be your guide. For those hot summer nights, serve over ice or throw it all in a blender. Warm up a wintry night by adding to fresh coffee or hot cocoa.

Tequila Mockingbird

JIG THE TEQUILA
HALF JIG THE GREEN CRÈME
DE MENTHE
TRIPLE JIG THE
SWEET-N-SOUR

HIGHBALL GLASS OR TALL COOL GLASS

Sweet. Yeah! Sour. Yeah! Mock-ing-bird. Yeah! Everybody, have you heard? You can make a Tequila Mockingbird. Just fly it all in a tall cool glass of ice, then if this Mockingbird don't make you sing, I'll find someone to buy you a diamond ring! And if that diamond ring don't shine, then I'll just make you another little drink of mine.

23

● ● ● ● ● ● ● ● ● ● ● ● ● ● ● ● ●

PONY THE RUM
PONY THE VODKA
PONY THE BANANA LIQUEUR
FILL WITH ORANGE JUICE
TALL COOL GLASS

Brass Funky Monkey

Hey, funky monkey! Start all this monkey business with a tall cool glass of ice. Swing in the rum, vodka, banana liqueur, and orange juice, beat your chest, and then stir with a straw. The Beastie Boys would go ape over this one!

HALF JIG THE VODKA
HALF JIG THE WHITE
CRÈME DE CACAO
HALF JIG THE GALLIANO
HALF JIG THE BANANA
LIQUEUR
FILL WITH ORANGE JUICE
TALL COOL GLASS

A little bird told me that this tweet little concoction would have you chirping in the trees! Fly everything into a tall cool glass of ice, garnish with some fancy fruit, then say, "Bye-bye, birdie!"

● ● ● ● ● ● ● ● ● ● ● ● ● ● ● ●

OUNCE THE CROWN ROYAL
CANADIAN WHISKEY
OUNCE THE CHAMBORD
FILL WITH CRANBERRY
JUICE
TALL COOL GLASS

No cages or boiling water for this little lobster! Rock the whiskey, liqueur, and cranberry juice in a tall juicy glass and garnish with a big fat straw. It tastes so good that soon you'll be clawing for another one.

JIG THE CRÈME DE NOYAUX
JIG THE WHITE CRÈME
DE CACAO
HALF JIG THE VANILLA-
FLAVORED VODKA
DOUBLE JIG THE CREAM
MARTINI GLASS

Y ou'll want to gather and store this potable liquid right into a shaker tin filled with ice. Shake it up and strain into a martini glass. Sit back and enjoy, but don't hibernate too long, little squirrel, because it will soon be time to gather more nuts!

25

• • • • • • • • • • • • • • • • •

DOUBLE OUNCE THE VODKA
CUPA GINGER BEER
DOUBLE OUNCE THE
LIME JUICE
COPPER CUP

D on't be stubborn, cool mule! Try this strong classic creation of vodka, lime juice, and ginger beer. You can kick it in a tall cool glass, but it's meant to be enjoyed in a copper cup. Don't worry, it won't make you sterile!

**QUARTER JIG THE COFFEE
LIQUEUR
QUARTER JIG THE
IRISH CREAM
QUARTER JIG THE CROWN
ROYAL CANADIAN WHISKEY
SHOT GLASS OR PONY GLASS**

Donald
DuckFart

I know the name of this creation quacks you up but a coupla these and everything will roll off your back. Waddle over and find a shot glass, then layer in the order given. When you replace the whiskey with Grand Marnier, it's called a B-52. Just thought you'd like to know, little ducky!

• • • • • • • • • • • • • • • • • • • •

Great
White
Shark Bite

**HALF JIG THE VODKA
HALF JIG THE RUM
HALF JIG THE TRIPLE SEC
HALF JIG THE IRISH CREAM
HALF JIG THE GODIVA
WHITE CHOCOLATE LIQUEUR
FILL WITH CREAM
TALL COOL GLASS**

G et ready to swim with the big sharks, little fishy! Attack a tall cool glass of ice, and coast in all the white goodness. Mix it up, then let your jaws do the judging.

How Now, Brown Cow

DOUBLE JIG THE COFFEE LIQUEUR

FILL WITH MILK

HIGHBALL GLASS

How Now, Brown Cow! This yummy libation of coffee liqueur and milk is simply mooooovelous! For a summertime treat, try it in the blender and for a cold wintry night, try it in coffee.

• • • • • • • • • • • • • • • • • • •

JIG THE BLACKBERRY BRANDY

HALF JIG THE WHITE CRÈME DE MENTHE

ROCKS GLASS

Bumblebee Stinger

Beeeeeeeeeware! This little potion has a sting! Buzz the blackberry brandy and white crème de menthe over a rocks glass of ice then bumble it around. Take a break from your busy day, rest those little wings, and be Queen Bee for a day.

**JIG THE VODKA
FILL WITH EQUAL PARTS
OF PINEAPPLE AND
GRAPEFRUIT JUICE
HALF JIG THE GRENADINE
TALL COOL GLASS**

Josie and the Pink Pussycats

Think pink! This yummy Pussycat will have you purring like a kitten. Scratch up a tall cool glass of ice and playfully purr— I mean, pour—everything in, then stir. Soon you'll be able to answer the question "What's new, pussycat?"

● ● ● ● ● ● ● ● ● ● ● ● ● ● ● ●

See Ya Later, Alligator

**JIG THE COCONUT RUM
HALF JIG THE MELON
LIQUEUR
HALF JIG THE RASPBERRY
LIQUEUR
HALF JIG THE JÄGERMEISTER
FILL WITH PINEAPPLE JUICE
TALL COOL GLASS**

Wrestle up a tall cool glass of ice and slap in everything. Stir it up good, add a fancy fruit garnish and a straw, then I'll see ya later, alligator!

Dead Green Frog

**QUARTER JIG THE
COFFEE LIQUEUR
QUARTER JIG THE GREEN
CRÈME DE MENTHE
QUARTER JIG THE IRISH CREAM
QUARTER JIG THE VODKA
DOUBLE JIG THE CREAM
HIGHBALL GLASS**

You won't find any warts on this little frogger! First, hop the vodka and cream in a highball glass of ice. Next hop the rest of the ingredients and your Dead Green Frog will appear right before your blinking eyes. Kiss a coupla these, and you'll probably see Prince Charming sooner than you think!

To cool yourself down on a hot muggy night, pour this frog in a blender. What's green and travels at 80 m.p.h.?

29

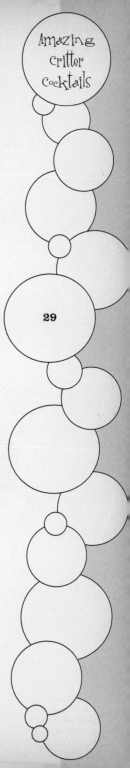

JIG THE DARK RUM
HALF JIG THE WHITE RUM
HALF JIG THE BRANDY
SPLASHA GRENADINE
FILL WITH EQUAL PARTS OF
ORANGE JUICE AND
SWEET-N-SOUR
TALL COOL GLASS

Desert Scorpion Sunset

This Scorpion is deadly! Mix its venom in a tall cool glass of ice, and you'll feel it sting after just one sip! Garnish with some juicy fruit and crawl away into the night, you nocturnal species, you.

• • • • • • • • • • • • • • • • • • • •

Who Let the salty Dogs Out?

JIG THE VODKA
FILL WITH GRAPEFRUIT JUICE
FRESH SLICED LIME AND SALT
HIGHBALL GLASS OR A TALL
COOL GLASS

Who let the dogs out? Sniff up a glass and rim it with the lime then dip it into the salt. Next, fill the glass with ice, then pour in the vodka and grapefruit juice. For a salt-free tail wagger, just add the vodka and grapefruit juice and the drink turns into a Greyhound. You'll be bowwowing in no time at all, little doggy!

(Pink grapefruit juice is nice too!)

Hairy Vanilla Gorilla Milk

JIG THE VANILLA-
FLAVORED VODKA
HALF JIG THE
COFFEE LIQUEUR
HALF JIG THE IRISH CREAM
HALF JIG THE BANANA LIQUEUR
TRIPLE JIG THE CREAM
TALL COOL GLASS

You'll go ape over this wild concoction! Swing all the ingredients into a tall cool glass of ice, and stir it up, little monkey. Be forewarned: This jungle juice has been known to bring out the beast in you!

31

Killer Blue Whale Tail

JIG THE VODKA
JIG THE BLUE CURAÇAO
DOUBLE OUNCE THE
ORANGE JUICE
DOUBLE OUNCE THE PINEAPPLE JUICE
DOUBLE OUNCE THE SWEET-N-SOUR
TALL COOL GLASS

This is one whale you'll want to save! Grab a tall cool glass of ice, and fill it with all the ingredients listed above. Now flip it into a shaker tin, and let it all go swimming. Flip it back into the tall cool glass, and garnish with some fancy fruit. Stick in a straw, suck with your blowhole, and soon you'll feel like Free Willy!

JIG THE VODKA
JIG THE COFFEE LIQUEUR
FILL WITH MILK
DOUBLE SPLASHA COLA
TALL COOL GLASS

Colorado
Bulldog

If a dog is man's best friend, then you just found a new friend! Pour in the vodka, coffee liqueur, and milk into a tall cool glass. Stir it up, then add the cola on top. Soon you'll be showing your puppy-dog eyes.

32

Awesome Quick-Draw Shots and Shooters

The Coolest and Hippest Shots and Shooters in the Galaxy

Get ready for the ride of your life, space cowboy! Let those nimble fingers do the walking through the next few pages, and you'll discover the most awesome quick-draw shots and shooters in the galaxy. Check out the rounds of hard-to-find attention-gettin', layered, slammin', chuggin', and flaming cosmic concoctions on the planet! While visitin', don't feel like you're under the gun and go shootin' your foot off by gettin' behind the wheel of a car. Let someone else lead the wagon train.

Devil With a Blue Kamikaze Dress On

**JIG THE VODKA
HALF JIG THE
BLUE CURAÇAO
HALF JIG
THE LIME JUICE
FLOAT THE 151 PROOF RUM
MATCHES
MARTINI GLASS OR SHOOTER GLASS**

Fe-fe, fi-fi, fo-fo, fum. Look out everybody, here it comes! Fe-fe, fi-fi, fo-fo, fum, pour everything in a shaker save the rum. Strain it all nice in a martini glass. Now float the rum and light that Devil! Blow out the flame, then suck it all down 'cause it's not too skinny and not too fat. It's a real humdinger, and you'll like it like that.

• • • • • • • • • • •

Disco Ball Inferno

**JIG THE GOLDSCHLAGER
TONGUE THE POP ROCKS
SHOT GLASS**

Hey, disco babe! Swirl that bottle of Goldschlager, watching the gold sparkle around and around like a disco ball. (If you're the dramatic type, hold a

flashlight up to it in a dark room for the full effect.) Pour the shiny gold liquid in a shot glass, pop some of your favorite Pop Rocks on your tongue, and shoot to feel the dancing inferno in your mouth. Burn, baby, burn. I promise you won't explode!

● ● ● ● ● ● ● ● ● ● ● ● ● ● ● ● ●

Magic Rainbow Lemon Drops

QUAD JIG THE CITRUS-FLAVORED VODKA
DOUBLE JIG THE TRIPLE SEC
SIX-OUNCE THE SWEET-N-SOUR
DOUBLE SPOONA SUGAR
SLICE THE LEMON
PACK OF FOOD COLORING
PRETTY SHOOTER GLASSES

35

Somewhere over the rainbow you'll find a colorful row of magic Lemon Drops. Rub the lemon slice on the rims of four shooter glasses, then dip them in the sugar. Now secretly add a drop of food coloring into the glasses, then catch a shaker tin of ice. Fill the shaker with the citrus-flavored vodka, triple sec, and sweet-n-sour. (Get ready, here comes the magic.) Strain into the glasses, and watch everyone freak out when each shooter turns out a different color. They are magically delicious as well!

Flaming Dr Pepper

THREE-QUARTER
JIG THE AMARETTO
QUARTER JIG THE
151 PROOF RUM
HALF A GLASS OF BEER
MATCHES
SHOT GLASS

This may be an old slammer to some, but not if you're twenty-one! Pour up half a glass of beer, then reach for a shot glass and fill with amaretto and rum. Ready for the fun? Okay, light the shot, drop it in the beer, then chug it all back. They say that it tastes like Dr Pepper. What do *you* say?

**BOTTLE OF RED CINNAMON
SCHNAPPS
EMPTY HALF-GALLON
MILK CARTON
H₂O
SHOT GLASSES MADE OF ICE**

Fire and
Ice-Ice Baby

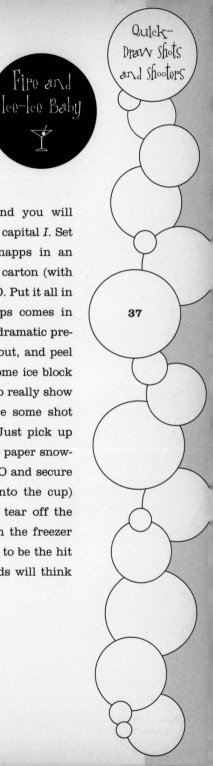

Serve up this oxymoron, and you will impress your friends with a capital *I*. Set a bottle of red cinnamon schnapps in an empty half-gallon milk or juice carton (with the top cut off), then fill with H₂O. Put it all in the freezer. (Cinnamon schnapps comes in clear or red; use red for a more dramatic presentation.) When ready, take it out, and peel off the carton to see your awesome ice block frozen around the bottle. Cool! To really show off your frozen talents, prepare some shot glasses made of ice; it's easy! Just pick up some paper Dixie cups and some paper snow-cone cups. Fill the cups with H₂O and secure the cones (pointed end down into the cup) with duct tape. Let 'em freeze, tear off the paper, and arrange on a tray in the freezer until they are needed. Get ready to be the hit of the party, because your friends will think you are the coolest!

37

Blow Job

**HALF JIG THE COFFEE
LIQUEUR
HALF JIG THE IRISH CREAM
TOP WITH WHIPPED CREAM
SHOT GLASS OR PONY GLASS**

This ambiguous shot is great for birthdays, bachelorette parties, or just for fun. Listen up! Here's whatcha do: Grab a shot glass or pony glass (Miss Charming's favorite glass), and pour in the coffee liqueur. Next, layer the Irish cream on top of the coffee liqueur, then top it with whipped cream (add a stemless maraschino on top if the drinker is a virgin to this shot). Here comes the fun! The person doing the shot puts his or her hands behind their back, leans down, and licks and sucks out the whipped cream. He or she then wraps their mouth around the glass, taking it back and swallowing the shot (don't forget to swallow). Then the drinker sets the glass back down. Are you the most popular person in the room? Well, if you weren't before, then you are now!

**JIG THE TEQUILA
SPRINKLE OF SALT
LIME WEDGE
SHOT GLASS**

Tequila Passion Shot

Here's a shot that's limited only by your imagination! Pour up a shot of tequila, then lick your partner's wrist and sprinkle some salt on it. Next, place a lime wedge in your partner's mouth (meat side out). Now lick the salt, shoot the tequila, and bite into the juicy lime, ending this passion shot with a kiss. Where's the imagination? you ask. Well, there can be other places to put the salt, tequila, and lime. You do have an imagination, don'tcha?

Even American Girls Get the Red, White, and Blues

**PONY THE WHITE CRÈME
DE CACAO
SPLASHA GRENADINE
FLOAT THE BLUE CURAÇAO
SHOT GLASS OR PONY GLASS**

Miss Charming has personally served thousands of these tasty patriotic shots! Grab a shot or pony glass, and fill it with the white crème de cacao. Next, dribble the grenadine, and watch it sink to the bottom. Now float the blue curaçao on top, and admire this beautiful shot. Shoot it all at once, and your taste buds will be amazed at how it tastes exactly like a chocolate-covered cherry!

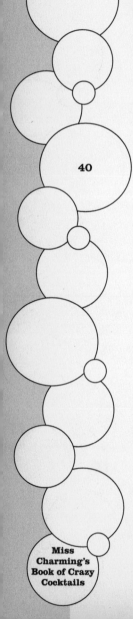

Slammer

JIG YOUR FAVORITE LIQUOR
TRIPLE OUNCE THE 7UP
COVER WITH COCKTAIL
NAPKIN
HIGHBALL GLASS

Here's a popular shot that's been around a long time. Just pour your favorite liquor in a sturdy highball glass, add the 7UP, and place a cocktail napkin on top. Here comes the slamming part. Slam the highball down *hard* then chug it while it's fizzing. You're a grand slammer now!

• • • • • • • • • • • • • • • • •

HALF JIG THE APPLEJACK
HALF JIG THE TUACA
SPLASHA CINNAMON
SCHNAPPS
CAN OF WHIPPED CREAM
SHOT GLASS

Apple Pie in the Face

You don't have to work the pie-throwing booth at the carnival to get a pie in your face! Fill a shot glass with the applejack, Tuaca, and cinnamon schnapps, then hold it in one hand. In your other hand, grab the can of whipped cream, shoot the shot, and spray the white fluff in your pie hole. Tastes just like apple pie!

JIG THE 151 PROOF RUM
DASHA COFFEE LIQUEUR
DASHA CREAM
LIGHTER
STRAW
SHOT GLASS

Bong
Hit

H ere's a bong hit you can get high on in public! In a shot glass dash the coffee liqueur and cream, then fill with rum (looks like bong water—at least that's what they tell me, wink-wink). Light the shot and let it burn a few seconds, then blow it out. Inhale it down your throat, then cover the empty shot glass with your hand. Now slip the straw in between your thumb and forefinger and suck the 151 fumes captured in the glass and it will make you cough.

41

Upside-Down Woo Woo

**JIG THE VODKA
HALF JIG THE
PEACH SCHNAPPS
TRIPLE OUNCE THE
CRANBERRY JUICE
SHAKER TIN AND STRAINER**

An upside-down shooter? You better believe it! Take a shaker tin of ice, and fill it with the vodka, peach schnapps, and cranberry juice. Place a strainer on top of the shaker, then have your partner lay his head back and open his mouth. Now swirl the shaker tin around and strain the Woo Woo straight into his upside-down mouth!

At a party you can fill up any cocktail in an empty liquor bottle with a pourer on top and give everyone upside-down Margaritas, Cosmopolitans, Lemon Drops, or whatever you want.

42

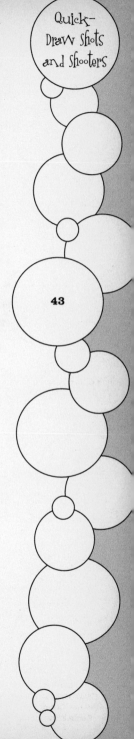

THIRD JIG THE 151
PROOF RUM
THIRD JIG THE
JÄGERMEISTER
THIRD JIG
THE RUMPLE MINZE
SHOT GLASS

Liquid
Cocaine

This shot is incredibly popular! Pour the rum, Jägermeister, and Rumple Minze in a shot glass, then shoot it down your throat. This is only for the hardcore shot lovers!

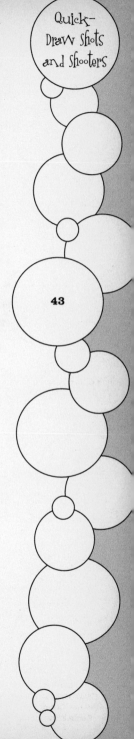

Quick-
Draw Shots
and Shooters

43

**HALF CUPA PEACH
SCHNAPPS
HALF CUPA VODKA
LARGE BOX OF
ORANGE JELL-O
CUPA BOILING H$_2$O
SMALL PAPER NUT CUPS**

Hairy
Fuzzy-Navel
Jell-O Shots

Ever wondered how to make those spiked Jell-O shots? It's easy! Basically all you have to do is replace the "cold" water part of the recipe with alcohol. (Something Mrs. Cleaver never tried!) Don't stop there. . . . Let your imagination jiggle! Try making Whiskey or Amaretto Sour shots with lemon Jell-O. Or Margarita shots with tequila and lime Jell-O. How about Sex on the Beach shots with vodka, peach schnapps, and orange and cranberry Jell-O? The most popular way to serve these jigglers is in paper nut cups (they have them at party stores) because it makes it easy to squeeze them into your mouth. But you can also serve them in fancy glasses with spoons, too, or small paper 3-ounce Dixie cups. Come on! Let's get jiggy wit' it!

**HALF JIG THE BUTTERSCOTCH
SCHNAPPS
HALF JIG THE IRISH CREAM
TWO MARASCHINO CHERRIES
PONY OR SHOT GLASS**

Buttery
Pierced Nipple

This shot is probably the yummiest shot, to date. In a shot or pony glass pour in the butterscotch schnapps, then pull off the stem from one of the cherries (looks like a pierced nipple), then drop it into the butterscotch schnapps. Next, layer the Irish cream on top of the schnapps, using the other cherry. Simply hold the cherry by the stem and lower it into the shot glass, barely touching the surface of the schnapps. Now pour the Irish cream on the cherry so that it breaks the fall of the Irish cream, then raise the cherry, keeping it on the surface as the level rises. You just learned how to get layered! Now you're ready to experience a Buttery Pierced Nipple. It goes down like butta!

45

JIG THE BERRY-FLAVORED VODKA

HALF JIG THE RASPBERRY LIQUEUR

JIG THE SWEET-N-SOUR

JIG THE PINEAPPLE JUICE

MARTINI GLASS OR SHOOTER GLASS

Purple People-Eater Hooter Shooter

Watch out purple people-eaters, here's one hooter shooter you'll fall in love with! Throw the berry-flavored vodka, raspberry liqueur, sweet-n-sour, and pineapple juice in a shaker tin of ice and shake it up like a one-eyed, one-horned, flying purple people-eater. Strain it "violetly" into a martini glass, then drink it up!

● ● ● ● ● ● ● ● ● ● ● ● ● ● ● ● ● ● ●

Key Lime Margarita Sour Power

JIG THE KEY LIME CREAM LIQUEUR

HALF JIG THE TEQUILA

HALF JIG THE MELON LIQUEUR

TRIPLE JIG THE SWEET-N-SOUR

LIME SLICE

MARTINI OR SHOOTER GLASS

Just the mention of key lime conjures up images of Florida. And if you've ever wondered what Florida *tastes* like, then look no further, little dreamer. Rim a martini glass with a lime slice, then grab a shaker tin of ice and pour in all the ingredients. Shake it up, then strain into the glass. Mmmmm, sweet, tart, and delicious; it's better than eating sand and salt water!

● ● ● ● ● ● ● ● ● ● ● ● ● ● ● ●

**JIG THE BLACK VODKA
HALF JIG THE ROMANA
SAMBUCA BLACK
HALF JIG THE
BANANA LIQUEUR
MARTINI GLASS**

Ha, ha! Mojo Jojo laughs at your pain! He is bad, he is evil, he is Mojo Jojo. Not only will he try to target the Powerpuff Girls, he will target you with this lawbreaking concoction. Grab a villainous shaker tin, and swindle all the ingredients around like a monkey taking over the world. Strain it nicely into a shooter glass, and get ready to feel the wrath. Ahhhh, revenge never tasted so sweet!

47

HALF JIG THE 151 PROOF RUM

JIG THE MELON LIQUEUR

JIG THE COCONUT RUM

HALF JIG THE SLOE GIN

JIG THE GOLDSCHLAGER

TRIPLE JIG THE ORANGE JUICE

TRIPLE JIG THE PINEAPPLE JUICE

FANCY FRUIT

TALL COOL GLASS OR HURRICANE GLASS

SHOT GLASS

Somewhere over the Rainbow

You'll find a real pot of gold at the end of this rainbow! Fill a tall cool glass with ice and pour in the rum and melon liqueur. In a shaker tin of ice add the coconut rum, orange juice, and pineapple juice, then shake and strain very slowly into the glass, being very careful not to mix it completely with the melon liqueur. Now float the sloe gin on top, garnish with some fancy fruit, and you have a beautiful rainbow. Next, fill the shot glass with Goldschlager, and set it next to the rainbow. When you're finished drinking the rainbow you get to shoot the pot of gold. Who needs a wizard with a drink like this?

END-OF-THE-NIGHT BAR MAT SHOOTER GLASS

Matador

I know that all of you high-volume night-club/danceclub bartenders out there are asking yourself, "Is she really going to tell the world about one of our little secrets?" Well, the answer is . . . why not? The *Matador* is the spillage that is collected on a bartender's bar mat. Not the floor mat, silly. It's the mat on top of the bar where all the drinks are made. I've known several reasons why some people drink the complimentary *Matador*, but most of them are late-night drunken bets and twenty-first birthdays.

Bodacious Boy Toy Concoctions

Testosterone-Inspired Libations for the Men from Mars

Hey, guys! I know that the fastest way to a man's heart is through his gullet, so here are some concoctions to get your engine started. You'll find all kinds of macho Bodacious Boy Toy Concoctions overflowing with masculinity! Just remember that after getting your game on with these libations, the only seat in the car you are allowed to ride in is the backseat, or shotgun, hot rod!

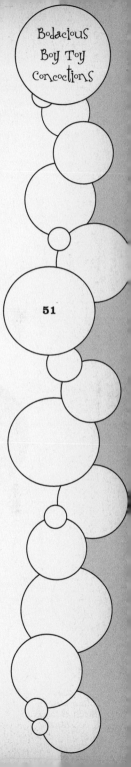

'57 T-Bird with Hawaiian License Plates at the Drive-In

JIG THE
SOUTHERN COMFORT
HALF JIG THE AMARETTO
HALF JIG THE
GRAND MARNIER
FILL WITH
PINEAPPLE JUICE,
MANGO JUICE, AND
SWEET-N-SOUR
LONG EXTENSION CORD
TELEVISION WITH BUILT-IN VCR
POPCORN
TALL COOL GLASS

51

Try this wildly popular roadster in a tall cool glass of ice at the movies! Just pour in the Southern Comfort, amaretto, and Grand Marnier, then fill with equal amounts of pineapple juice, mango juice, and sweet-n-sour. Carry your television with a built-in VCR out to the hood of your car, and plug it in. You now have your own '57 T-Bird with Hawaiian License Plates at the Drive-In. The only thing to decide now is what movie to watch.

By the way, for all of you guys who ask me all the time about cute little surprises to do for the girl in your life . . . well, this is one of them, lover boy.

HALF JIG THE JACK DANIEL'S
HALF JIG THE YUKON JACK
JIG THE ROOT-BEER
SCHNAPPS
FILL WITH COLA
TALL COOL GLASS

Jackhammer

Fill your air-pressured pistons with this high-speed concoction of Jack Daniel's, Yukon Jack, root-beer schnapps, and cola. Nozzle this speed into a tall cool glass of ice, stick in a straw, and mix it by drilling the straw up and down just like a jackhammer, muscle man.

● ● ● ● ● ● ● ● ● ● ● ● ● ● ● ● ● ●

The Man Show Brew

YOUR FAVORITE ICE-COLD BEER
PEEKABOO NUDIE-GIRL
GLASSES (THE KIND WITH
THE PICTURES OF LADIES WHO
STRIP NAKED WHEN
A COLD BEVERAGE IS
POURED INTO THE GLASS)

If you're not talented enough to have a weekly show like Jimmy and Adam do, then make your own! Rustle up an ice-cold six-pack, with a six-pack ring made out of beef jerky and some girlie peekaboo glasses, then you'll have your very own "man show" going on. Ziggy-Zaga, Ziggy-Zaga! Oy! Oy! Oy!

You'll find girlie glasses @ ebay.com and spencergifts.com.

Hit Me With Your Best Shot

151 PROOF RUM
COCONUT RUM
PEACH SCHNAPPS
PINEAPPLE JUICE
SQUIRT GUNS
SOAKER GUN

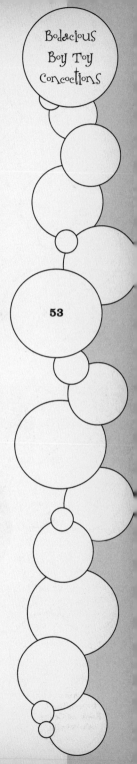

R eady to be the life of the pool party? Whip up this great-tasting, stain-free concoction, and fill a soaker with it. Pump the soaker softly, then walk around your wildest party giving everybody a shot straight in the mouth! To be a really cool host, have some pre-filled squirt guns chillin' in the fridge or in a cooler of ice to hand out to your guests. Try sterilizing your double kitchen sink and put the hooch in one side so that guests can refill their guns. The other side of the sink can be used to wash their hands before and after filling up their guns. Also, try your own stain-free, pulp-free, quick-draw recipes and you'll be the hippest and coolest host of any pool party!

JIG THE IRISH CREAM
JIG THE LIME JUICE
TWO SHOT GLASSES

Cement Mixer

This is a great gag shot! The combination of the Irish cream and the lime juice in your mouth makes it feel really, really weird, but don't tell your victim this. Have your buddy shoot the Irish cream first, instructing her not to swallow. Then have her shoot the lime juice, swishing it all around in her mouth with the Irish cream. The citrus in the lime juice curdles the cream and will begin to feel very strange in her mouth. You and your friends will be quite entertained watching your victim's face as she experiences the Cement Mixer!

● ● ● ● ● ● ● ● ● ● ● ● ● ● ● ● ● ● ●

Antifreeze

JIG THE MELON LIQUEUR
JIG THE LEMON-FLAVORED
VODKA
FILL WITH 7UP
TALL COOL GLASS

To keep from boiling over, protect your cooling system with this toxic liquid. In a tall cool glass of ice add the melon liqueur and lemon-flavored vodka, then fill with 7UP. You'll feel the difference in your engine right away!

Cordless Screwdriver

JIG THE MANDARIN-
FLAVORED VODKA
QUARTER JIG THE TRIPLE SEC
HALF AN ORANGE SLICE
PACKET OF SUGAR
DRIBBLE THE 151 PROOF RUM
MATCHES
SHOT GLASS

Grab your tools and drill that vodka and triple sec over ice in a shaker. Shake it up, and manually pour it into the shot glass, then set the half orange slice on top. Now dump the sugar on the orange, dribble some of the rum on the sweetness, and light that baby. When the flame dies down, lift the orange, slam the shot, then bite into the warm, sweet orange slice, sugar lips. Mmmm!

JIG THE 151 PROOF RUM
PONY THE AMARETTO
PONY THE MELON LIQUEUR
FILL WITH PINEAPPLE JUICE
TALL COOL GLASS

Hand Grenade XM84

If any of you guys have ever been in the U.S. Army, then you know that the Grenade XM84 is designed to confuse and disorient. Pour this diversionary device in a tall cool glass of ice, mix it up, pull the pin, then watch out, soldier, because I want you to survive this blow!

HALF OUNCE THE IRISH WHISKEY

HALF OUNCE THE IRISH CREAM

PINT THE GUINNESS

SHOT GLASS AND PINT GLASS

Irish Car Bomb

Y ou don't even have to be a wee bit Irish or be in an Irish pub to enjoy this popular slammer! Grab a shot glass filled Irish whiskey and Irish cream. Fill a pint glass with Guinness, drop in the shot, then chug it all back at once. Soon you'll begin to feel what it's really like to be Irish!

Agent Orange

JIG THE MANDARIN-FLAVORED VODKA

HALF JIG THE GRAND MARNIER

HALF JIG THE COINTREAU

FILL WITH ORANGE JUICE

TALL COOL GLASS

B e careful with this toxic herbicide, because it will mess you up a long time after it gets into your system! Grab a tall cool glass and fill with the mandarin-flavored vodka, Grand Marnier, Cointreau, and orange juice. Then drink it up, military man!

B-52 Bomber

HALF JIG THE COFFEE LIQUEUR
HALF JIG THE IRISH CREAM
HALF JIG THE GRAND MARNIER
PONY OR SHOT GLASS

This flying classic shot has always been the bomb! Reach for a shot glass and pour in the coffee liqueur. Now layer the Irish cream, then layer the Grand Marnier on top of the Irish cream. Come on, jet-setter, time to test your wings!

● ● ● ● ● ● ● ● ● ● ● ● ● ● ● ● ●

Sidekick Sidecar

JIG THE COGNAC
HALF JIG THE COINTREAU
JIG THE SWEET-N-SOUR
ROCKS GLASS OR MARTINI GLASS

What ever happened to the sidecar? You know the kind that's attached to motor-cycles? Batman and Robin had one. Mayberry's Andy and Barney had one. And now you can have one. If you like to travel hard and fast, then shake it all up in a shaker and strain into a martini glass. If you prefer the slow scenic route, pour everything over ice. Hope you enjoy this blast from the past, sidekick!

Traffic Light

JIG THE VODKA
JIG THE MELON LIQUEUR
JIG THE SLOE GIN
DOUBLE OUNCE THE
SWEET-N-SOUR
DOUBLE OUNCE THE ORANGE
JUICE
TALL COOL GLASS

Pull up to this Traffic Light, and get ready to rev your engine! Reach for an idle tall cool glass of ice, and pour in the vodka and melon liqueur (got your green light). Next, with caution, fill the glass mosta the way with the orange juice and the sweet-n-sour (got your yellow light). Lastly, float the sloe gin on top (got your red light). Ready, set, go, dragster!

Atomic Bomb

HALF JIG THE VODKA
HALF JIG THE GIN
HALF JIG THE PEACH SCHNAPPS
HALF JIG THE CINNAMON SCHNAPPS
HALF JIG THE 151 PROOF RUM
MATCHES
MARTINI GLASS OR SHOOTER GLASS

This uranium shooter is destructive! Grab a lethal shaker tin of ice and add the vodka, gin, peach schnapps, and cinnamon schnapps. Shake this deadly combination gently, then strain into a shooter glass. Float the rum on top, then light this A-Bomb! Wait until the flame dies down, then shoot. Be careful, because a few of these could cause serious damage!

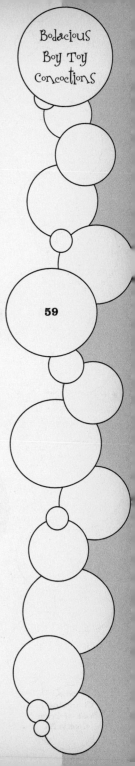

Bodacious Boy Toy Concoctions

JIG THE GALLIANO
JIG THE WHITE CRÈME DE CACAO
TRIPLE JIG THE CREAM
MARTINI GLASS, HIGHBALL GLASS, OR TALL COOL GLASS

Golden Cadillac

I don't want to scam you with this Cadillac, so I want you to know up front that it's pretty sweet, has low mileage, and really looks better on a lady. If you decide to take it out for a test drive, then I suggest you drive it on the rocks. Just mix up all this fuel over ice, and the ride will be smooth. If you're buying it for a lady, then shake it up and strain it into a martini glass, handsome!

● ● ● ● ● ● ● ● ● ● ● ● ● ● ●

Titanium Crowbar

HALF JIG THE CROWN ROYAL CANADIAN WHISKEY
HALF JIG THE 151 PROOF RUM
HALF JIG THE GOLDSCHLAGER
SHOT GLASS

Here's an industrial-strength metal tool that can really do some damage! Pry open the lids of the whiskey, rum, and Goldschlager, then pour an even amount of each into a shot glass. Be careful with this

Crowbar, because the titanium makes it stronger than a standard steel bar, providing maximum leverage!

●●●●●●●●●●●●●●

Lube Job

HALF JIG THE VODKA
HALF JIG THE IRISH CREAM
SHOT GLASS

Lubricate your chassis and all your moving joints by pumping vodka and Irish cream into a shot glass, then shooting. Once this preventative grease reaches your front and rear suspensions, you'll feel like new, grease monkey!

HALF JIG THE RUM

HALF JIG THE COFFEE LIQUEUR

HALF JIG THE IRISH CREAM

HALF JIG THE AMARETTO

HALF JIG THE FRANGELICO

DOUBLE JIG THE PIÑA COLADA MIX

TALL COOL GLASS

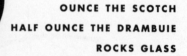

Bushwhacker

You'll be the master of the bush after you learn how to make this Bushwhacker! Take your machete out of its sheath and clear a path to that blender of yours, then throw in all the ingredients. Push the highest-speed button you can find with those strong fingers, and blend it up good. Pour it in a tall cool glass. All the vines and thickets from your mind will soon be cut away!

Rusty Nail

OUNCE THE SCOTCH

HALF OUNCE THE DRAMBUIE

ROCKS GLASS

Didn't your mama tell you not to play around rusty nails because you might step on one? Well, you're all grown up now (hopefully), and you can play around all you want with this Rusty Nail! Mix the scotch and Drambuie in a rocks glass over ice, and we'll soon see what you're made of, big boy.

Liquid Panty Remover

HALF JIG THE
SOUTHERN COMFORT
HALF JIG THE PEACH
SCHNAPPS
HALF JIG THE AMARETTO
HALF JIG THE SLOE GIN
HALF JIG THE VODKA
FILL WITH CRANBERRY JUICE
AND ORANGE JUICE
TALL COOL GLASS

You love looking at Victoria's Secret panties, but I know the real secret you're after is how to get them removed! Try making this Liquid Panty Remover for the chick you dig. Grab a tall cool glass of ice and pour in the Southern Comfort, peach schnapps, amaretto, vodka, and sloe gin, then fill with cranberry and orange juice and stir. You now have ingredients from popular drinks named Scarlett O'Hara, Woo Woo, Screwdriver, Fuzzy Navel, and Sloe Comfortable Screw. With this combination, how could you *not* get those panties off?

HALF JIG THE SAMBUCA
HALF JIG THE COFFEE LIQUEUR
HALF JIG THE BANANA LIQUEUR
HALF JIG THE BLUE CURAÇAO
DOUBLE JIG THE MILK
SPRINKLE THE CINNAMON
TWO STRAWS CONNECTED TOGETHER
SIX SHOT GLASSES
MATCHES
MARTINI GLASS

Flaming Blue Lamborghini

Here's one Lamborghini you'll be able to afford! Start fueling up by grabbing a martini glass, six shot glasses, and two straws. Line up the shot glasses, then fill them up in this order: half jig Sambuca, half jig coffee liqueur, half jig banana liqueur, half jig blue curaçao, jig o' milk, jig o' milk. Put two straws together, have some matches handy, and set out the martini glass. Now you're ready to start the engine. Pour in the Sambuca, then light. Swirl it around to keep the flame from going out, then add the coffee liqueur, banana liqueur, and the blue curaçao. While the flame is still burning, sprinkle the cinnamon, and it will sparkle. (Looks cool when the lights are low.) Now take the double straw, pour in the two jigs of milk, and suck it down. Time to shift up to fifth gear, baby!

Excellent Name-Dropper Cocktails

Cocktails You Can Call Out by Name

If I pulled the names Tom Collins, Rob Roy, and Scarlett O'Hara out of a hat, what would you guess they all have in common? I'm not just name-dropping to impress you folks; they are popular cocktails! Just remember not to get behind the wheel of a car with Freddy Fudpucker, Harvey Wallbanger, and Joe Swinger, because someone might end up Bloody Mary!

JIG THE VODKA

HALF JIG THE DARK CRÈME DE CACAO

HALF JIG THE BUTTERSCOTCH SCHNAPPS

HALF JIG THE IRISH CREAM

FILL WITH CREAM

TALL COOL GLASS

Willy Wonka's Whammy

The Oompa Loompas came up with this little Whammy right after that golden-ticket fiasco! Reach for a tall cool glass of ice and add all the ingredients, then stir. Mmmmmm! It's also Wonkarific in the blender!

● ● ● ● ● ● ● ● ● ●

John Collins

JIG THE WHISKEY

FILL WITH SWEET-N-SOUR

AND CLUB SODA

TALL COOL GLASS

John Collins is Tom Collins's little brother that you don't hear about too often. Rumor has it that he lives in the Tennessee mountains, and he likes it that way. Secretly grab a tall cool glass of ice, pour in the whiskey and equal parts of sweet-n-sour and club soda, then stir. Make like a hermit in a holler and enjoy this laid-back relative!

A Very Merry Shirley Temple

OUNCE THE VANILLA-
FLAVORED VODKA
HALF OUNCE THE CHERRY
BRANDY
FILL WITH 7UP
DOUBLE DASHA GRENADINE
TALL COOL GLASS

This Shirley Temple will curl your hair! Tap up a tall cool glass of ice, and roll in the vanilla-flavored vodka, cherry brandy, 7UP, and grenadine, then let your talent tickle your taste buds!

● ● ● ● ● ● ● ● ● ● ● ● ● ● ● ●

Lady Godiva's Nude Martini

OUNCE THE GODIVA WHITE
CHOCOLATE LIQUEUR
OUNCE THE VANILLA-
FLAVORED VODKA
DOUBLE OUNCE THE CREAM

Do you think your taxes are too high, but *don't* think that you can pull off a naked ride through your town on a barebacked white horse in protest? Then this is the drink for you! Grab that shaker tin of ice, and pour in the Godiva White Chocolate Liqueur, vanilla-flavored vodka, and cream, then ride that shaker hard. Strain it into a martini glass, then say, "Giddy-up, horsey!"

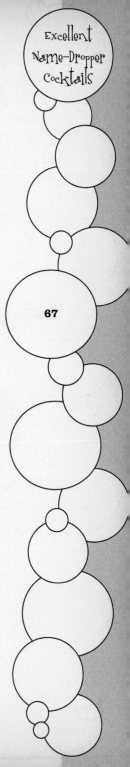

JIG THE VODKA

FILL WITH CLAMATO JUICE

DOUBLE DASHA TABASCO

TRIPLE DASHA

WORCESTERSHIRE

TEASPOONA FRESH LIME JUICE

STALK OF CELERY

TALL COOL GLASS

Hail Caesar

Do as the Romans do, and capture all the ingredients in a soldier-tall glass. Garnish with celery and raise your glass in victory, proclaiming your accomplishment. Hail, Caesar! Hail, Caesar!

Scarlett O'Hara

JIG THE SOUTHERN COMFORT

FILL WITH CRANBERRY JUICE

TALL COOL GLASS

This charming concoction will have you delightfully spoiled! Manipulate a tall cool glass of ice and passionately add the Southern Comfort, then fill with cranberry juice. A couple of these southern treats and you'll be gone with the wind!

Beam Me Up. Scotty

**THIRD JIG THE
COFFEE LIQUEUR
THIRD JIG THE
BANANA LIQUEUR
THIRD JIG THE IRISH CREAM
SHOT GLASS**

Have this famous chief engineer beam you up at light speed! Just grab a shot glass and pour in equal amounts of coffee liqueur, banana liqueur, and Irish cream. Get ready to put your hands in Scotty's endless resourcefulness, and shoot it back, *Star Trek* fan!

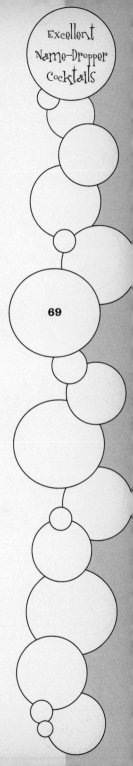

JIG THE VODKA
FILL WITH STORE-BOUGHT
BLOODY MARY MIX
SUPPLEMENT WITH A DASH
STEAK SAUCE (MISS
CHARMING'S SECRET
INGREDIENT), TABASCO,
WORCESTERSHIRE, AND FRESH-
SQUEEZED LIME
GARNISH WITH WHAT TICKLES YOUR
FANCY: CELERY, LIME, SALTED RIM,
OLIVES, SCALLION, PICKLED OKRA, GREEN
BEAN, OR A PEPPEROCHINI

Bloody
Mary

The classic Bloody Mary wins hands down for the most popular early to midday cocktail choice, but it can also be enjoyed any ole hour of the day! Grab a tall cool glass of ice, then add all your favorite ingredients. If you replace the vodka with tequila, this spicy little number turns into a Bloody Maria. And if you add a parasol and a spoonful of sugar, it turns into a Bloody Mary Poppins!

JIG THE VODKA
FLOAT THE GALLIANO
FILL WITH ORANGE JUICE

Harvey Wallbanger

Harry Headbanger said that his cousin, Harvey Wallbanger, has always been a big hit with the ladies. To find out if this is true, just fill a tall cool glass of ice with the vodka and orange juice, then bang the Galliano on top. Are you ready for Harvey to have his way with you, ladies?

FYI—a drink made with vodka, Southern Comfort, sloe gin, and orange juice is called a Sloe Comfortable Screw. If you add Galliano, it's called a Sloe Comfortable Screw Up Against the Wall.

71

● ● ● ● ● ● ● ● ● ● ● ● ● ● ● ● ● ● ●

Jack-in-the-Box

PONY THE APPLEJACK
PONY THE JACK DANIEL'S
PONY THE YUKON JACK
FILL WITH PINEAPPLE JUICE
AND SWEET-N-SOUR
SPLASHA GRENADINE
TALL COOL GLASS

Don't let this Jack-in-the-Box scare you! Just chase it all into a tall cool glass of ice and crank it around and around with a straw. After all of this fun, pop! it down your weasel!

OUNCE THE CROWN ROYAL
CANADIAN WHISKEY
HALF OUNCE THE
CHAMBORD
FILL WITH CRANBERRY JUICE
AND 7UP
TALL COOL GLASS

Queen Elizabeth 2

Her nickname is *QE2,* and she sails the ocean blue. Start the smooth sailing by ordering the Crown Royal, Chambord, and equal parts of cranberry juice and 7UP into a tall cool glass of ice, then rock that boat with a straw. Her Royal Majesty would serve nothing less at a Bon Voyage party aboard the *QE2*!

• • • • • • • • • • • • • • • • • •

Rob Roy

DOUBLE JIG THE SCOTCH
THREE-QUARTER JIG THE
SWEET RED VERMOUTH
GARNISH WITH A
MARASCHINO CHERRY
HIGHBALL GLASS

This red-haired Scottish hero would've been proud to know that Americans named a drink after him two hundred years after his death. In a highball glass of ice pour in the scotch, sweet red vermouth, and drop in the cherry, then sit back and enjoy this little sipper.

**HALF OUNCE THE MELON
LIQUEUR
HALF OUNCE THE
PEPPERMINT SCHNAPPS
HALF OUNCE
THE JÄGERMEISTER
SHOT OR PONY GLASS**

When you're in a laid-back reggae mood, try this buffalo soldier! Rasta up a shot glass, and pour in the melon liqueur. Layer the peppermint schnapps on top of the melon liqueur, then the Jägermeister on top of the schnapps. Throw on that dreadlock wig, and you be livin' de life, mon!

• • • • • • • • • • • • • • • • •

**JIG THE GIN
QUARTER JIG THE FRESH-
SQUEEZED LIME JUICE
QUARTER JIG THE FRESH-
SQUEEZED LEMON JUICE
FILL WITH CLUB SODA AND 7UP
HIGHBALL GLASS**

This new twist on the Gin Rickey might make you take your clothes off and go dancing in the rain! Grab a highball glass and dance in the gin and fresh-squeezed juices, then fill with equal amounts of soda water and 7UP. You're livin' *la vida loca* now, baby!

73

OUNCE THE BRANDY

HALF OUNCE THE WHITE CRÈME DE CACAO

HALF OUNCE THE COFFEE LIQUEUR

DOUBLE OUNCE THE CREAM

SPRINKLE THE NUTMEG

MARTINI GLASS

Brandy Alexander the Great

Let Alexander the Great conquer you with this delicious cocktail! Demand a shaker tin of ice, then add the brandy, white crème de cacao, coffee liqueur, and cream. Shake it up like an army that's hungry for a fight, then strain it into a martini glass. Sprinkle the top with nutmeg, sit back, and work out your daily strategies.

George Bush

**JIG THE GEORGE DICKEL
BOURBON
HALF GLASS OF BUSCH BEER
PINT GLASS
SHOT GLASS**

This forty-third president of the United States doesn't drink anymore, so he won't be consuming any of these, but *you* can! Just drop a shot of George Dickel Bourbon into a Busch beer, then chug it back. Soon you'll be seeing the Stars and Stripes with these amber waves of grain!

● ● ● ● ● ● ● ● ● ● ● ● ● ● ● ● ●

Freddy Fudpucker

**JIG THE TEQUILA
HALF JIG THE GALLIANO
FILL WITH ORANGE JUICE
TALL COOL GLASS**

It's your lucky day because ya ain't been pucked 'til you've been fudpucked by Freddy Fudpucker! Chuck the tequila, Galliano, and orange juice in a tall cool glass, then suck. Then ask yourself, "If a woodchuck could chuck wood, how much wood would a woodchuck puck?"

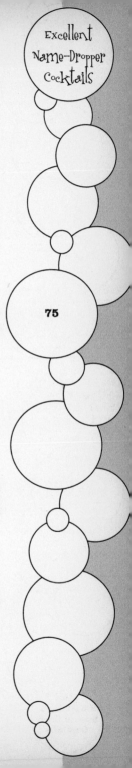

**JIG THE AMARETTO
SPLASHA MELON LIQUEUR
FILL WITH EQUAL PARTS OF
SWEET-N-SOUR AND
ORANGE JUICE
TALL COOL GLASS**

Joe
Swinger

Come cool your tongue and ease your mind from a stressed-out crazy world, hepcat! Groove on over to a tall cool glass of ice in your swanky bachelor pad, and swing in the amaretto, melon liqueur, and equal parts of sweet-n-sour and orange juice. You're set to cha-cha now, baybeeeeee!

DOUBLE JIG THE VODKA

HALF JIG THE DE KUYPER

SOUR APPLE PUCKER

SCHNAPPS

HALF JIG THE COINTREAU

THREE-QUARTER JIG THE FRESH LEMON

JUICE

GRANNY APPLE SLICE

CHILLED MARTINI GLASS

Dale's Big Sour Apple Martini

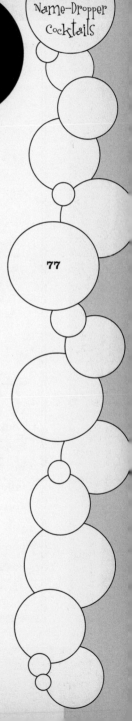

D ale "King Cocktail" Degroff is the most famous bartender in New York City, and it doesn't surprise me that one of his most popular recipes is named after the Big Apple. Take a shaker tin of ice and pour in the vodka, Sour Apple Pucker, Cointreau, and fresh lime juice, then shake it up well. Strain it into a chilled martini glass, then garnish with a green Granny apple slice. Pucker up those lips, baby, and enjoy the freshest drink in New York City!

Totally Cool College Cocktails and Shooters

Luscious Libations Filled with Colorful Team Spirit!

Ra, Ra, Ree! Kick 'em in the knee! Ra, Ra, Rass! Kick 'em in the other knee! Looking for some hard-to-find spirited college cocktails? Then take a halftime and get into the spirit with Totally Cool College Cocktails and Shooters. You'll find creative team and school color-related concoctions to try at your next party or local hangout. And while you're in college gettin' an education, remember that it's not smart to drink and drive, sports fan.

UNIVERSITY OF FLORIDA GATORS

Gator Chomp

PONY THE MANDARIN-FLAVORED VODKA

HALF PONY THE BLUE CURAÇAO

TRIPLE PONY THE FRESH-SQUEEZED FLORIDA ORANGE JUICE

HIGHBALL GLASS

SHOT GLASS

79

This number-one party school says, "It's Great to Be a Florida Gator!" Just ask Albert the Alligator or Mr. Two Bits! Tackle a tall cool glass, and pour the Florida orange juice (there's the Orange). Grab a shaker of ice, scoring it with the mandarin-flavored vodka and blue curaçao (there's the Blue), and slap it around like you're wrestling a Gator. Strain into a shot glass and set inside the highball. Got your Orange, got your Blue, and got your game on, so slam that baby down, and I'll see ya later, alligator! Gooooo, Gators!

**JIG THE COCONUT RUM FOR
THE CALIFORNIA BEACH BUM
JIG THE GOLD TEQUILA
HALF JIG THE BLUE CURAÇAO
JIG THE CREAM OF COCONUT
FILL WITH PINEAPPLE JUICE AND
CREAM
TALL COOL GLASS**

Bearly
Sober

Hey, Bruins! This inebriating beverage will attack and put down a Trojan! Score a tall cool half glass of ice with the coconut rum, blue curaçao, cream of coconut, pineapple juice, and cream, and stir (got your Light Blue). Drop in a shot of gold tequila (got your Gold), and you're ready to sing the Mighty Bruin song, praise John Wooden, and then get to sippin'. Gooooo, UCLA!

UNIVERSITY OF GEORGIA BULLDOGS

Uga Chuga

ONE CAN OF RED BULL
ENERGY DRINK
HALF OUNCE THE
BLACK VODKA
HALF OUNCE THE
JÄGERMEISTER
TALL COOL GLASS
SHOT GLASS

You'll feel like running around the Battle of the Hedges after slamming this energetic slammer! Pop that Red Bull can and pour it in a tall glass (got your Red). Now fill a shot glass with the black vodka and Jägermeister (got your Black) and drop that baby in the Red Bull. Chug that Uga, then bark like a dog. Gooooo, Dogs!

81

ARIZONA STATE UNIVERSITY SUN DEVILS

JIG THE 151 PROOF RUM
SPLASHA BANANA LIQUEUR
SIX-OUNCE THE RX POWER
HERBAL PUNCH (ARIZONA
BEVERAGE COMPANY)
TEASPOON
MATCHES
TALL COOL GLASS
SHOT GLASS

Fill a tall cool glass halfway with chilled Arizona Tea brand Rx Power Herbal Punch (got your Red). Now, in the shot glass, splash in some banana liqueur, then fill with rum (got your Gold). Light the shot, then pick up the teaspoon and tap the glass several times, making a ringing bell sound. Drop the flaming gold Sun Devil in the tall cool glass, then chug it all back. Now you should feel like going to the stadium and ringing the real ASU bell! Gooooo, Gold!

UNIVERSITY OF NORTH CAROLINA TAR HEELS

Tar Heel Hamma Rama Slama

JIG THE GODIVA WHITE CHOCOLATE LIQUEUR
HALF JIG THE VODKA
HALF JIG THE 151 PROOF RUM
HALF JIG THE BLUE CURAÇAO
DOUBLE JIG THE CREAM
MARTINI GLASS OR SHOOTER GLASS

They say that God must have been a Tar Heel because he made the sky Carolina Blue. Well, I don't know about that, but this Carolina shooter sure tastes like heaven with a kick! Pour everything in a shaker tin with ice, then shake-shake that baby all over the place. Strain it all into a martini glass, then slama that Carolina Blue. UNC Rules!

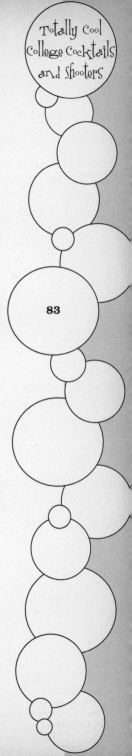

83

LOUISIANA STATE UNIVERSITY TIGERS

HALF JIG THE VODKA

HALF JIG THE BANANA LIQUEUR

DOUBLE DROP OF BLUE CURAÇAO

DOUBLE DROP OF GRENADINE

SHORT COCKTAIL STIRRER

TWO SHOT GLASSES

Hey, Bayou Bengals! They'll have to put you in a cage just like Mike the Tiger after a few of these wild concoctions! In a shot glass pour half a jig of banana liqueur (that's your Yellow). In another shot glass half jig the vodka, and drop the grenadine and blue curaçao, then stir (that's your Purple). Now layer the Purple on top of the Yellow, sing "Hold That Tiger," then shoot that baby back quick. Gooooo, Tigers!

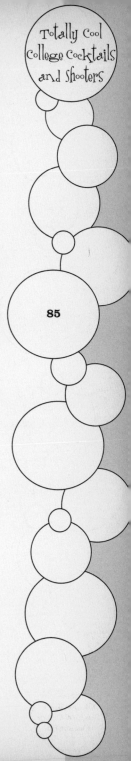

UNIVERSITY OF COLORADO BUFFALOES

Tough Buff

JIG THE VODKA
JIG THE COFFEE LIQUEUR
ORANGE JUICE
TALL COOL GLASS

85

Hey, Buffs! You'll be able to push that big buffalo out on the field all by yourself after a coupla these! Grab a tall cool glass of ice, and jig the vodka and coffee liqueur (there's your Black). Slowly add the orange juice (there's your Gold), and stick in a straw. Your Boulder taste buds will be jumping for joy because this Tough Buff tastes exactly like a Tootsie Roll. Sweet! Gooooo, Buffs!

UNIVERSITY OF TENNESSEE VOLUNTEERS

JIG THE MANDARIN-FLAVORED VODKA
HALF JIG THE JACK DANIEL'S
DOUBLE JIG THE ORANGE JUICE
TONGUE THE POP ROCKS
HIGHBALL GLASS

Hey there, Vols! Get ready to Rock 'n' Vol with this exploding orange shooter! Roll everything but the Pop Rocks into a shaker tin of ice, then shake, rattle, and roll that sucker. Strain it all into a highball glass, sing "Rocky Top," put some Pop Rocks on your tongue, then slam it down. Smokey the Dog would even like this one! Goooooooo, Vols!

UNIVERSITY OF
NEBRASKA CORNHUSKERS

Tailgater Husker Hooch

BOTTLE OF VANILLA-
FLAVORED VODKA
BOTTLE OF
SOUTHERN COMFORT
BOTTLE OF SLOE GIN
BOTTLE OF AMARETTO
FILL WITH CRANBERRY AND
ORANGE JUICE
BAG OF ICE
LARGE STAND-UP COOLER WITH A SPOUT
PLASTIC CUPS

G et the Husker Fever and throw all this barking juice in a big cooler (got your Red). Grab a coupla Husker fans and shake it up good, baby. Soon you'll be as spirited as Herbie Husker on game night! GO, BIG RED!

OHIO STATE UNIVERSITY BUCKEYES

JIG THE VODKA
JIG THE RUM
FILL WITH TROPICAL-
PUNCH GATORADE
TALL COOL GLASS

High Buckeyes! Here's a sporty concoction that even Brutus would like. Mix everything up in a tall cool glass (got your Scarlet) and soon you'll feel like high-steppin' it out on the field just like the tuba player dottin' the *i*! Gooooo, Buckeyes!

UNIVERSITY OF MICHIGAN WOLVERINES

JIG THE VODKA
JIG THE GALLIANO
SPLASHA BLUE CURAÇAO
DOUBLE JIG THE ORANGE
JUICE
HIGHBALL GLASS
SHOT GLASS

Wolverines are known for their strength and endurance, and you're going to need it for this strong shooter! Gather up a highball and a shot glass. Score the highball with the chilled and strained Galliano and orange juice (got your Maize), and then score the shot glass with the chilled and strained vodka and blue curaçao (got your Blue). Set the shot glass into the highball, sing, "Hail to the Victors," then open your jaw and slam! You're ready for the "Big House" now. Gooooo, Blue!

UNIVERSITY OF ALABAMA CRIMSON TIDE

JIG THE OUZO
RED LICORICE TWIZZLER
ROCKS GLASS

Roll Tide Suicide

Big Al says one suck of this powerful Tide will knock you over! Splash the ouzo in a rocks glass of ice, then stir and the ouzo will turn white (got your White). Now bite the two ends off of a red licorice Twizzler (got your Red) so that you can use it as a straw. Yell, "Rama Jama, Yella Hamma, Give 'Em Hell, Alabama!" then suck it all at once with the Twizzler straw. Roll, Tide, Roll!

UNIVERSITY OF WASHINGTON HUSKIES

HALF JIG THE GOLDSCHLAGER

HALF JIG THE PEPPERMINT SCHNAPPS

DROP OF BLUE CURAÇAO

DROP OF GRENADINE

TWO SHOT GLASSES

Bow down to Washington, and tackle two shot glasses. In one, half jig the Goldschlager (got your Gold). In the other, half jig the peppermint schnapps, one drop of grenadine, one drop of blue curaçao, and stir (got your Purple). Slowly layer the Purple on top of the Gold, sing, "Bow Down to Washington," and shoot like a malamute! Gooooo, Huskies!

TULANE UNIVERSITY GREEN WAVE

HALF A GLASS OF PILSNER BEER (YELLOW BEER)

JIG THE CITRUS-FLAVORED VODKA

DOUBLE SPLASHA BLUE CURAÇAO

Hey, Tulane! Get ripped by making a big splash with this Green Wave libation. Drop and splash a shot of citrus-flavored vodka and the blue curaçao in half a glass of beer, and watch it turn olive green right before your little Pelican eyes. Say, "Roll, Green Wave, Roll," then slurp it all back. Gooooo, Olive and Blue!

PENN STATE
NITTANY LIONS

Untamed Lion

JIG THE **151** PROOF RUM

HALF JIG THE BLUE CURAÇAO

SPLASHA LIME JUICE

TRIPLE JIG THE **7**UP

ONE COCKTAIL NAPKIN

HIGHBALL GLASS

Slam a coupla these Lions, and it won't matter that there aren't any names on the Penn State jerseys! Get your school Blue on by scoring the rum, blue curaçao, lime juice, and 7UP in a highball. Place a napkin over the drink then slam that cool cat, making it fizz all over the place. Now chug it down your throat, Lion lover! We ARE . . . Penn State!

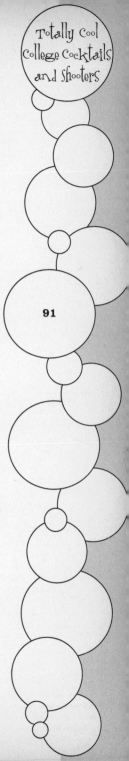

Totally Cool College Cocktails and Shooters

91

JIG THE GOLD TEQUILA

HALF JIG THE GRAND MARNIER

PACKET OF SUGAR

SLICE OF ORANGE

SPLASHA ORANGE JUICE

MATCHES

SAUCER

SHOT GLASS

Longhorn
Cannon Shooter

92

Get ready to light up with this burnt-orange Cannon Shooter! Rustle up a shaker tin of ice, and score it with the gold tequila and splasha orange juice and strain it into the shot glass. Now grab that saucer, lay down the orange slice, put the packet of sugar on top, half jig the Grand Marnier, and light that citrus, baby! When the flame goes down, hold up the "Hook 'em, Horns" hand signal, shoot the gold tequila, then bite into the warm sugary burnt orange slice. Wait a minute, Longhorn . . . you're not done yet! Now pour the remaining Grand Marnier from the saucer into the shot glass and chase that shooter. By now you should feel like banging five-hundred-pound Big Bertha! Hook 'em, Horns!

UNIVERSITY OF SOUTH CAROLINA GAMECOCKS

Cock Blocker

**JIG THE BLACK VODKA
HALF GLASS OF
CRANBERRY JUICE
TALL COOL GLASS
SHOT GLASS**

Hey, let's give a cheer. Carolina is here! Fill a tall cool glass halfway with cranberry juice (got your Garnet) then drop in the black vodka (got your Black). Now give a big Carolina cheer, and slam back that cocky cocktail! Soon you'll be running around like a chicken with your head cut off! Gooooo, Cocks!

93

PURDUE UNIVERSITY BOILERMAKERS

**JIG THE GOLDSCHLAGER
PINT THE GUINNESS
PINT GLASS
SHOT GLASS**

Black and Gold Boilermaker

This Boilermaker may sound different, but Rowdy and Pete think it's really tasty! Pour up a pint of Guinness (got your Black) and drop in a shot of Goldschlager (got your Gold). Now chug that baby faster than a locomotive that is maintained by the Reamer Club at full speed. Oh, yeah! Gooooo, Purdue!

AUBURN UNIVERSITY TIGERS

DOUBLE JIG THE MANDARIN-FLAVORED VODKA
JIG THE BLUE CURAÇAO
QUAD OUNCE THE ORANGE JUICE
DOUBLE OUNCE THE 7UP
THREE BOTTOM-HEAVY HIGHBALL GLASSES

Tiger Striper

Everyone is confused about Auburn's mascot (except AU, that is). Are they the Tigers? Or are they the War Eagles? Maybe they are the Plainsmen? Well, I'm here to set the record straight. The answer is, Tigers! But the other mascots are part of AU, too, so I'm honoring all three. Grab three highball glasses, and set 'em out, Tiger. Now score a shaker tin with ice, mandarin-flavored vodka, and the orange juice. Strain into two of the highballs (got your Orange). Now jig the blue curaçao and 7UP in the remaining highball (got your Blue). Okay, Auburn, lean in and listen closely, because you are about to stripe the Tiger! Grab the Blue highball and set it on the rim of one of the Orange highballs at eight o'clock. When it is balanced, grab the remaining Orange highball and set it on the rim of the Blue highball at four o'clock. Now you have your Tiger Stripes! After everyone is amazed at your balancing ability, do the War

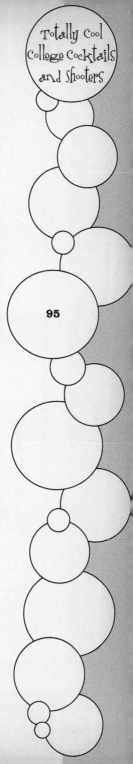

Eagle Battle Cry, and slam all three highballs in consecutive order. Gooooo, Tigers! (It will feel really weird balancing the glasses at first, but it's very scientific. Just practice it a few times to get the feel, and soon you'll be an all-star highball stacker. I bet even Aubie could do it!)

FLORIDA STATE UNIVERSITY SEMINOLES

Seminole Slam

**PONY THE GOLDSCHLAGER
HALF PONY THE
CHAMBORD
SMALL COCKTAIL STRAW
SHOT GLASS**

Tell the bartender on Tennessee Street to shake that Goldschlager bottle, then pony into a shot glass (got your Gold). Half pony the Chambord (got your Garnet). Do the Tomahawk Chop and throw that baby down your throat faster than a Seminole Spear. Gooooo, 'Noles!

Fabulous Picture Show Cocktails

Famous Cocktails Seen on the Silver Screen

Lights! Camera! Action! Step past the velvet rope and get ready to shake, stir, and lemon twist your way to becoming the star of your very own cocktail show! Miss Charming's Fabulous Picture Show Cocktails will have you making the luscious libations you've seen in the movies, and they are guaranteed to win a standing ovation! After the show, just make sure that the only automobile you get into is on a movie set!

Elvis Presley, Angela Lansbury

JIG THE WHITE RUM
JIG THE BLUE
CURAÇAO
FLOAT HALF A JIG
OF DARK RUM
FILL WITH PINEAPPLE
JUICE AND
SWEET-N-SOUR
TALL COOL GLASS

Blue
Hawaii
Mai Tai
(1961)

97

Mai Tai one on, and take the white rum, blue curaçao, and equal parts of pineapple juice and sweet-n-sour on a trip to a tall tropical glass of ice paradise, Hawaiian style! Do the hula, moving your hips just like Elvis would, while stirring it up. Float with yummy dark rum, then garnish with a juicy slice of pineapple speared with a cherry and a pretty paper parasol. I can't help falling in love with this tropical treat! Aloha!

The Big Lebowski White Russian (1998)

JIG THE COFFEE LIQUEUR

JIG THE VODKA

FILL WITH CREAM

HIGHBALL GLASS

98

Hey, dude, if you are the ultimate slacker who wakes up one day with gangsters peeing on your rug, then this is the drink for you. Kidnap a highball glass of ice, and visit it with the coffee liqueur, vodka, and cream. No entangled, mistaken identity here. Just watch the toes!

DOUBLE JIG THE JACK DANIEL'S
SOUR MASH BOURBON
SIX SPRIGS OF FRESH MINT
TRIPLE OUNCE THE SUGAR
WATER
MUDDLER
CRUSHED ICE
TALL COOL GLASS

Goldfinger Mint Julep (1964)

A James Bond film with horses? No other cocktail would do but a Mint Julep! James requests it with sour mash and a little on the sweet side, so grow the mint out back and stock the bourbon within. Start by dropping in five of the sprigs (leaving one sprig for a garnish) in the bottom of the tall cool glass, then add half the sugar water (sugar water is just sugar mixed together with water). Next, take the muddler and crush up the mint so that it releases all its invigorating oils together with the sugar water. Mmmmmm. Now fill completely with crushed ice, add the bourbon, and fill with the rest of the sugar water, adding a little bit more water if needed, then garnish with a mint sprig. You're ready for the horse races now!

Sean Connery

Fabulous Picture Show cocktails

99

Bette Midler, Barbara Hershey

**JIG THE BRANDY
HALF JIG THE WHITE
CRÈME DE MENTHE
ROCKS GLASS**

Beaches
Stinger
(1988)

Here's a drink that will last a lifetime! Mix these two friends of brandy and white crème de menthe in a rocks glass filled with ice, and it will be the start of a lifetime friendship. A coupla these, and you'll soon feel the wind beneath your wings!

100

Al Pacino, John Cazale, Robert De Niro

JIG THE RUM
JIG THE BANANA LIQUEUR
WHOLE BANANA
QUARTER CUPA CREAM
CUPA ICE
TALL COOL GLASS

The
Godfather, Part
II Banana
Daiquiri
(1974)

101

Fredo, the second son of Don Corleone, has a sweet, childlike nature about him, so it doesn't surprise me that he orders a Banana Daiquiri in *The Godfather, Part II*. Start by putting everything into a blender, then make things happen by a push of a button. Pour it into a tall cool glass, stick in a straw, and enjoy like a Mafia king on vacation.

DOUBLE JIG

THE SWEET

VERMOUTH

ROCKS GLASS

Groundhog Day Sweet Vermouth on the Rocks (1993)

102

One could sip this drink over and over and over just like weatherman Bill Murray did in this sweet romantic comedy. When Groundhog Day rolls around, reach for a rocks glass of ice and pour in the sweet vermouth. You can now fall into your own time warp, little gopher!

Pam Grier, Samuel L. Jackson

JIG THE VODKA
FILL WITH
ORANGE JUICE
TALL COOL GLASS

Jackie Brown Screwdriver (1997)

While you're sitting around wondering what you're going to do with your million-dollar payoff, smuggle a tall glass of ice and fill it with the vodka and orange juice. Just don't fall in love with your bail bondsman!

JIG THE TEQUILA
HALF JIG THE TRIPLE SEC
DOUBLE JIG THE
SWEET-N-SOUR
SPLASHA LIME JUICE
CUPA ICE
TALL COOL GLASS

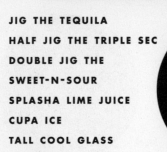

Boogie
Nights
Margarita
(1997)

W ho would've known that a seventies porn star's favorite drink was the Margarita? Skate all the Dirk Diggler special ingredients into a blender, then mix it up. Pour into a tall cool glass, and forget the salt because they didn't use it in the movie. Everyone is good at one special thing, ya know. Maybe making this Margarita is yours.

DOUBLE JIG

THE SAMBUCA

JIG THE VANILLA-
FLAVORED VODKA

DOUBLE SCOOP

THE VANILLA ICE CREAM

HALF CUPA MILK

TALL COOL GLASS

The
Adventures of
Ford Fairlane
Sambuca Milkshake
(1990)

105

Want to try Mr. "Rock 'n' Roll" Fairlane's favorite concoction? Make like a detective, and find the blender, adding one jig of sambuca, one jig of vanilla-flavored vodka, two scoops of ice cream, and the milk. Push some buttons on the blender and mix it up, baby. Pour in a tall cool glass, float with a jig of Sambuca, and light that frozen goodness. When the flame dies down, stick in a straw and enjoy, spy guy!

Due to the size of your scoops, you may have to experiment with the amount of milk used to get the right "milkshake" consistency.

**JIG THE RUM
DOUBLE JIG THE
SWEET-N-SOUR
FILL WITH SODA WATER
GARNISH WITH AN
ORANGE AND A
MARASCHINO CHERRY
TALL COOL GLASS**

Thunderball
Rum Collins
(1965)

106

For the first time, alcohol really saves Bond's life! Try your own silver-screen lifesaver by stealing a tall cool glass of ice and pouring in the rum, sweet-n-sour, and soda water. Stick in a straw and garnish with an orange and cherry. You might want to demand a ransom for this one!

Melanie Griffith

JIG THE DARK RUM
JIG THE WHITE RUM
FLOAT THE **151** PROOF
RUM
FILL WITH PINEAPPLE
AND ORANGE JUICE
SPLASHA GRENADINE
GARNISH WITH AN ORANGE SLICE
AND A MARASCHINO CHERRY
TALL COOL GLASS OR HURRICANE GLASS

Crazy
in Alabama
Hurricane
(1999)

107

Sometimes you have to lose your mind to find your freedom, and just one of these tropical libations will loosen up that mind! Pull a tall cool glass of ice, or better yet, a hurricane glass of ice, out of that hatbox, doll. Then pour in all the ingredients, save the 151 rum. Mix it all up then float the 151 rum. Garnish this glamorous concoction with an orange slice and cherry, then sit back and enjoy while you think about the pursuit of your dreams.

**OUNCE THE SEAGRAM'S
7 CROWN BLENDED
CANADIAN WHISKEY
FILL WITH 7UP
HIGHBALL GLASS**

*Saturday
Night Fever
7 & 7
(1977)*

108

G ot the night fever to be king of the dance floor? Start by ordering a 7 & 7 to help your disco inferno, baby. Just tell the bartender to grab a highball of ice and pour in the Seagram's 7 and 7UP. Soon we'll know just how deep is your love for this highball.

Tony Danza

JIG THE KAHLÚA
JIG THE DARK RUM
JIG THE **151** PROOF
RUM
JIG THE COCONUT CREAM
DOUBLE JIG THE
PINEAPPLE JUICE
DOUBLE JIG THE SWEET-N-SOUR
FANCY FRUIT
PAPER PARASOL
HULLED-OUT PINEAPPLE GLASS

She's out of control Double Kahlúa Punch (1989)

Ready for a major makeover? Hull out a pineapple to be used for your drinking container, then set aside. Walk over to the blender, and add the Kahlúa, dark rum, 151 proof rum, coconut cream, pineapple juice, and sweet-n-sour. Blend it all up, then pour into the pineapple. Stick in a straw, add some fancy fruit, and then stick in a paper parasol. Sure takes a lot of work for a makeover, but it's worth it!

JIG THE RUM
JIG THE BLUE CURAÇAO
HALF JIG THE TRIPLE SEC
DOUBLE JIG THE
PINEAPPLE JUICE
SHAKER TIN AND STRAINER
MARTINI GLASS

cocktail
Turquoise
Blue
(1988)

110

Do you want to shake, rattle, and roll just like Tom Cruise? Then put on an award-winning smile and grab a shaker tin of ice and pour in the rum, blue curaçao, triple sec, and pineapple juice. Shake it up like a glossy movie star, strain it into a martini glass, then wink. You've just learned one of the secrets of the trade!

● ● ● ● ● ● ● Jerry Lewis ● ● ● ● ● ● ●

DOUBLE OUNCE THE VODKA

DOUBLE OUNCE THE RUM

OUNCE THE GIN

HALF OUNCE THE SCOTCH

HALF OUNCE THE BRANDY

HALF OUNCE THE DRY VERMOUTH

SMIDGEN THE VINEGAR (THAT'S WHAT IT SAYS IN THE MOVIE!)

SPLASHA BITTERS

GARNISH WITH A LEMON PEEL, ORANGE PEEL, AND MARASCHINO CHERRY

VERY TALL COOL GLASS

The Nutty Professor Alaskan Polar Bear Heater (1963)

111

What a crazy drink! But it's what nerdy Professor Julius Kelp turned popular party animal Buddy Love orders at the hippest bar in town. Start with a very tall cool glass of ice and pour in all the ingredients of this potion, then mix it up nice. This elixir worked for Buddy in the chick chemistry department; maybe it'll work for you—at least until you pass out!

**DOUBLE JIG THE GIN
SPLASH THE DRY
VERMOUTH
GARNISH WITH TWO
SPEARED
COCKTAIL PEARL ONIONS
MARTINI GLASS**

The Net
Gibson
(1995)

112

In this film, Angela Bennett (Bullock) is looking for a man who's butch, beautiful, and brilliant—a Captain America–meets–Albert Schweitzer, who spends all day dashing into the fray while making the world safe for democracy and at night plays Bach cantatas while curing cancer. The man thing I can understand, but a Gibson on a tropical beach? Yuck! Oh well, it's just a movie, I guess. Grab a shaker tin of ice, adding the gin and dry vermouth. Shake it up good, then strain it into a martini glass. Drop in two speared cocktail onions and you're set to go, Cyberbob!

● ● ● ● ● James Stewart ● ● ● ● ●

QUARTER CUPA BRANDY
BOTTLE OF RED WINE
THREE CUPS OF WATER
ONE CUPA SUGAR
TWELVE CLOVES
TWO CINNAMON STICKS
STAINLESS-STEEL POT
CUPS

It's a
Wonderful Life
Mulled Wine
(1946)

66**M**ulled Wine, heavy on the cinnamon and light on the cloves, then off with you, m'lad, and be lively," says Clarence the angel. Try this vintage recipe while watching this timeless movie with your friends over the holiday season! In a stainless-steel pot add the water, sugar, cloves, and cinnamon sticks, and simmer for fifteen minutes. Then add the red wine, bringing it all to a drinkable temperature. Add the brandy, stir, and serve it to your holiday guests. It's a wonderful life!

113

JIG THE RUM

DOUBLE JIG THE CREAM OF
COCONUT

QUARTER CUPA
PINEAPPLE JUICE

JIG THE CREAM

SPOONA VANILLA
EXTRACT

CUPA ICE

GARNISH WITH A PINEAPPLE SLICE AND
MARASCHINO CHERRY

TALL COOL GLASS

Office
Space Piña
Colada
(1999)

114

I don't like my job, and I don't think I'll go anymore. You know I never really liked paying bills; I don't think I'm going to do that, either. How funny! And if your place of employment ever goes up in smoke, get away to a tropical beach and definitely order a Piña Colada! Grab the blender, and add all the ingredients, then push those tropical buttons, cubicle head. Pour it all into a tall cool glass, and garnish with a juicy pineapple slice and a maraschino cherry. Stick in a straw and get away from it all!

Ben Stiller, Robert De Niro

**JIG THE GIN
DOUBLE JIG THE
SWEET-N-SOUR
FILL WITH SODA WATER
TALL COOL GLASS**

Meet the Parents Tom Collins (2000)

First comes love. Then comes the interrogation. After all of that, I'd say it's time for a drink! Grab a tall cool glass of ice and travel in the gin, sweet-n-sour, and soda water, then sit back and enjoy this liquid lie detector!

GLASS OF CHAMPAGNE
BITTERS
SUGAR CUBE
CHAMPAGNE GLASS

Blast
from the Past
Champagne Cocktail
(1999)

116

You don't have to hide out in a bomb shelter for thirty-five years to try this classic bubbly treat! Just take a sugar cube and dash it a few times with bitters, then drop it into the bottom a champagne glass. Fill it with champagne, and you're ready for the end of the world. You don't even have to be a prostitute to drink it!

Fantabulous Special Occasion and Party Creations

Festive Libations for Cheerful Celebrations

These recipes serve thirty cool cats two servings each. If your friends are lushes, then pour more giggle juice, dude. If the serving amount is too large for your shindig, then do the math, party animal. Also, if there is a flavor you don't particularly like, don't sweat it. Just leave it out or replace it with something that does tickle your taste buds. It's all about having a good time. Also, the host or hostess with the mostest would never let their guests leave the party intoxicated, so have someplace for your guests to crash, even if it is a tent in the backyard!

Before you start flipping these pages, I want to give you a few hints and tips that will make you the best hostess cupcake ever!

KEEPING EVERYTHING COLD

Of course, you can always use ice to keep a punch cold, but it also waters it down. Try making an ice punch bowl by filling a large bowl with water then weighing down a medium-sized bowl so that the water comes up to the edge. (You can weigh it down with soup cans or even free weights.) Carefully set the bowls in the freezer, then when it's party time, pop off the bowls with a little warm water and add the punch. Set it on an attractive folded towel to absorb the water as the ice bowl melts. You can also keep a punch cold by setting a medium bowl into a larger bowl of ice. Other ways to keep all that goodness chilly are to float a chunk of ice cream in the punch, fill a plastic baggy with ice and let it float around the bowl, freeze a gelatin mold with mixer and place it in the punch, or use plastic ice that can be found in various stores that sell kitchen products. You can also look around for any containers that can be filled with water then frozen. I use frozen plastic gallon jugs for punches made in coolers, so that the mix is not diluted.

As for ice in the glasses, you can just use plain ole ice cubes, but what if you froze something cool into the cubes? The possibilities are endless: coffee beans, candy, olives, cherries, and anything else you can think of. *Also, you always want to begin by having your liquor and mixes cold, so store them in the fridge before the party.*

CREATIVE GLASSWARE

First, think about what kind of party you are throwing. There are so many things that you can use for glassware: hulled-out pumpkins, pineapples, or coconuts; small beach buckets; flower vases; large baby bottles; etc. Look around and you'll come up with all kinds of creative ideas! Don't forget to take advantage of all the really cool glass and plastic partyware that the discount stores carry in the summer. Thrift stores have a fantastic and diverse selection, and don't forget about the "Dollar Store"!

CREATIVE PUNCH CONTAINERS

If you own a punch bowl, great! If you don't, then open your eyes and look around. You'll discover containers you've never thought of before: coolers, storage bins, clean fish tanks, sterilized kitchen sinks, baby or toddler pool floats, large flowerpots, clean trash cans, children's plastic wagons or wheelbarrows, a plastic bag–lined large swim ring, inner tube or tire, a canning pot, baby pools, etc. Once, I used a plastic turtle-shaped sandbox. You'll never be able to walk through a store the same way again because you'll see things through different eyes and your imagination will come up with all kinds of ideas.

MEASURES

When your head is swimming with the correct amounts of booze and mixers to whip up in volume, think of a plastic gallon container as a large glass. A regular drink glass you would fill with a third of booze and the rest of the way with the mixer, right? So, just fill a gallon jug the same way. By the way, keeping a little collection of plastic gallon jugs is a must for an organized party giver. Making your punch ahead of time and keeping it nice and cool in the fridge is highly recommended!

FREEZE THE KEYS

To help in keeping intoxicated people off the road, try this: As everyone arrives at the party, have them throw their keys in a bowl of water, then add a heavy string with half of it in the bowl and the other half out of the bowl. Stick it in the freezer. When frozen, tie it up somewhere to thaw. Your guests are allowed to leave when their keys are unfrozen.

Who Wants to Be a Melonaire Punch?

BOTTLE OF MELON LIQUEUR

BOTTLE OF GOLD TEQUILA

HALF BOTTLE OF GRAND MARNIER

TWO GALLONS OF SWEET-N-SOUR

EMPTY MILK OR JUICE PINT CONTAINER

BIG PUNCH BOWL WITH LADLE

REAL OR FAKE MONEY

GOLD OR SILVER PLASTIC CUPS

Grab the game or turn on the tube, and invite all your millionaire wanna-bes over for an evening of fun! For liquid courage, add all the ingredients in a big punch bowl, and stir. To keep those millions cold, freeze a block of cold cash the night before, using an empty milk or juice container. Just add some bills, freeze, then float. You can add to the fun by freezing clean coins in ice-cube trays. Your guests will feel like royalty!

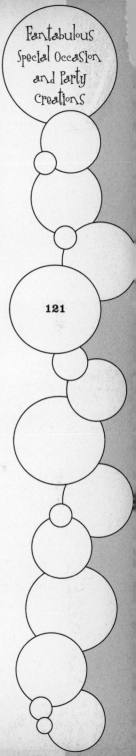

BOTTLE OF SOUTHERN COMFORT

BOTTLE OF COFFEE LIQUEUR

BOTTLE OF IRISH CREAM

TRIPLE JIG THE 151 PROOF RUM

DOUBLE GALLON OF MILK

FOUR CANS OF WHIPPED CREAM

FIVE-GALLON METAL BUCKET OR METAL CANNING POT

MATCHES

MASON JARS WITH HANDLES

Mason-Jar Blow Jobs

Looking for a way to warm up a group of friends on a cold, chilly night? Then round up a five-gallon metal container, and set it outside away from all things flammable. Start building your fire with the Southern Comfort, coffee liqueur, Irish cream, and two gallons of milk. Hand your friends the cans of whipped cream, and let them go crazy. Top off the heap with rum, then light that baby! After the flames die down, grab a mason jar by the handle and dip it into the liquid goodness. Everyone will be warmed up in no time!

Fried Copabanana Peanut Butter and Jamma

HALF BOTTLE OF
BANANA LIQUEUR
BOTTLE OF FRANGELICO
BOTTLE OF RASPBERRY
LIQUEUR
BOTTLE OF BERRY-
FLAVORED VODKA
DOUBLE JIG THE 151 PROOF RUM
DOUBLE GALLON OF MILK
FLOAT THE BANANA ICE CREAM
BIG PUNCH BOWL WITH LADLE
FESTIVE CUPS

Yeah, baby! Elvis is alive, and he wanted me to share his favorite party punch with you! Start taking care of business by pouring the banana liqueur, Frangelico, raspberry liqueur, berry-flavored vodka, and milk into a big punch bowl. Tenderly stir, then place the ice cream in the punch, adding the rum on top. Light that hunka-hunka burning banana love, baby, and soon your guests will not be able to help falling in love with this Fried Copabanana Peanut Butter and Jamma. Better set up a heartbreak hotel 'cause they won't be leaving the building any time soon!

**TEN BOTTLES OF DRY
CHAMPAGNE
BOTTLE OF CHAMBORD
RENT THE CHAMPAGNE
FOUNTAIN
PRETTY GLASSES**

Majestically
Luscious
Ambrosia Fountain

My guess is that Bacchus, the great god of wine, would serve nothing less than this delectable nectar of the gods at royal celebrations. Treat your guests like the gods they are by creating this flowing ambrosia. Rent a champagne fountain at a local party-rental store, and graciously pour in the dry champagne and bottle of Chambord. Set out pretty glasses around the fountain, and watch it become the center of attention.

124

Light
up the Night
With Spiced Black-
Light Delight

**BOTTLE OF SPICED RUM
BOTTLE OF CITRUS VODKA
BOTTLE OF YUKON JACK
DOUBLE GALLON OF PINK
LEMONADE
FIVE YELLOW HIGHLIGHTER MARKERS
FLORESCENT BLACK LIGHT
EXTRA-LARGE CLEAR BOWL
LARGE CLEAR BOWL WITH LADLE
LARGE FREEZER SPACE
CLEAR GLASSES/CUPS, GARNISHED WITH
GLOW STICKS**

Get ready to make this groovy boozy delight to impress all your psychedelic friends at your next glow party! You are going to make a glowing ice punch bowl, dude! Here's what to do: Set out an extra-large clear bowl, and fill it halfway with H_2O. Next, slip on some gloves and break open five yellow highlighter markers. Put the cottony stuff in the H_2O, squeeze out all the ink, then dispose of the cotton filler. Lay down a towel in a large freezer space, and set the bowl of highlighter H_2O on it. Now grab the large clear bowl and set it into the extra-large clear bowl. Push it down, and you'll see the highlighter H_2O rise up and around the sides to the top of the bowl. Listen up! *This is the way you want it to freeze to create a frozen glow bowl, so go find some heavy things around your house and weigh it down, baby!* After it's frozen and you're ready to get the party started, take the frozen glow bowl out of the freezer and pour in all the ingredients of the punch recipe. Don't forget to set out some clear glasses with glow sticks in them! Turn the lights down, flip the switch on the black light, and get ready for a totally cosmic experience!

If you can't find large clear bowls, then just use large clear storage bins. Remember, they need to be two different sizes. Also, get creative and put black light–active items around the punch bowl. Maybe even float some glow sticks in the punch.

Dew the Witches Brew

BOTTLE OF CRANBERRY-
FLAVORED VODKA
BOTTLE OF AMARETTO
TWO LITERS OF MOUNTAIN
DEW
GALLON OF PINEAPPLE JUICE
CUPA CRANBERRY JUICE
ONE OR TWO RUBBER GLOVES
BIG PUNCH BOWL WITH LADLE
CROCK-POT
DRY ICE (SEE NOTE BELOW)
SPOOKY GLASSES

When that spooky time of the year rolls around, just Dew the Witches Brew! The night before, fill up a rubber glove or two with cranberry juice, then freeze. Right before the party starts, scare up some cranberry-flavored vodka, amaretto, pineapple juice, and Mountain Dew, then pour it in a big punch bowl. Now tear off the rubber from the frozen cranberry juice, and you have a bloody hand to float around and keep the brew cold. Be a crafty little witch and set a Crock-Pot of warm water next to the punch bowl. Periodically add dry ice to the warm water to create a spooky foggy effect. For a killer dramatic effect, combine the dry-ice idea and the black-light-ice-punch-bowl idea used in the previous recipe. Your guests will really freak out, monster lover!

Note: Dry ice can be found in the Yellow

Pages under ice companies. It's frozen carbon dioxide (you know, the stuff you breathe out). Don't ever touch it with your bare hands, especially wet hands, unless you want a real bloody hand in the punch. Wear gloves or socks on your hands. Also, store it in a well-ventilated cooler or ice chest, not an airtight one (unless you're into explosions). The handling of the dry ice may sound scarier than Halloween itself, but if these simple precautions are followed, all will be fine.

TWO BOTTLES OF WHITE RUM

TWELVE PINEAPPLE JOLLY RANCHERS

GALLON OF PINEAPPLE JUICE

HALF GALLON OF COCO LOPEZ CREAM OF COCONUT

JIG THE VANILLA EXTRACT

LITER OF PINEAPPLE SODA

PINT OF VANILLA ICE CREAM

GARNISH WITH MARASCHINO CHERRY-SPEARED PINEAPPLE SLICES

BIG PUNCH BOWL WITH LADLE

Meanwhile, Back at the Jolly Rancher Punch

Hey, tropical cowboy! I'm gonna learn ya a whole new way of making yer own flavored rum. The night before the shindig, plop six of them pineapple Jolly Ranchers into a bottle of rum. Lo and behold, the next day you will have pineapple-flavored rum! Mercy! Now grab ya one of those tropical blenders, and mix up the rum, pineapple juice, coconut cream, and vanilla extract. (That crazy ole coconut cream won't act right 'til it's blended.) You'll be figurin' out real quick that not all of that will fit into that tiny tropical blender, so ya have ta do it in batches, partner. Don't worry, you'll figure it all out, cowboy! If you are blending ahead of time, just store it all in containers of some sort to keep it nice and cool in the fridge. I recommend taking this road: When the shindig is about to commence, pour it all in the punch bowl, add the pineapple soda, float the vanilla ice cream, then garnish the entire rim of the bowl with the maraschino cherry–speared pineapple slices. Ring that bell, and your friends will come callin', tropical cowboy!

If you can't find pineapple Jolly Ranchers, then cherry or strawberry will add a nice flavor to this here punch. Also, if you prefer to use vodka instead of rum, go for it! Never forget that the most important ingredient is yer imagination!

TWO BOTTLES OF BOONE'S
FARM STRAWBERRY WINE
BOTTLE OF MD 20/20
SEVEN BOTTLES OF RED WINE
CUPA BRANDY
HALF-GALLON OF ORANGE JUICE
HALF-GALLON OF CRANBERRY JUICE
EMPTY HALF-GALLON ORANGE JUICE
CONTAINER
FRUIT OF YOUR CHOICE (SLICED LIMES,
LEMONS, ORANGES, PEACHES, PINEAPPLE,
APPLES, AND GRAPES, BLUEBERRIES, OR
WHATEVER IS IN THE FRIDGE)
RED ROSES
BIG PUNCH BOWL WITH LADLE
WINEGLASSES

Spanish Harlem Night Sangria

The song says, "There is a rose in Spanish Harlem." And there are roses all around this Spanish Harlem Night Sangria! Serve this special sangria when the moon is on the run and the stars are gleaming. Mix the wine, brandy, and juices in a *grande* container, then pour into gallon jugs to keep cold in the fridge. Fill up the empty juice container with the sangria as well and freeze it into a sangria ice block. At fiesta time, pour the sangria in the bowl, add the sangria ice block, place a red rose on the block, and add some fruit. Surround the bowl with red roses and more fruit. Now crank up the Santana, Gloria Estefan, Jennifer Lopez, and Ricky Martin. ¡Ariba, amigo!

Sensational Peppermint-Patty Party Luge

BOTTLE OF PEPPERMINT SCHNAPPS
BOTTLE OF CHOCOLATE SYRUP
ICE LUGE

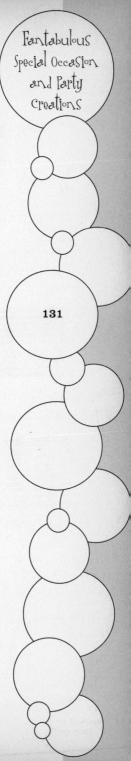

When I bite into this Peppermint Patty, I get the sensation that I can ski like an Olympian swishing down a mountain, the wind rushing through my hair as I pass an abominable snowman at breakneck speed, then breathtaking gold dust cascades down and around my glistening body. As I come out of this dream, I ask, "What the heck is a party luge?" Well, hang on to your earmuffs, snow bunny, because you are about to experience the icy ride of your life! An ice luge can be purchased at most ice companies. It's the rave! Basically, it's a block of ice in which they drill a hole and then put a clear tube in the hole. At the top, someone pours a shot of liquor as you put your mouth at the bottom of the luge and catch the icy shot in your mouth. With this recipe, you squirt some chocolate syrup in your mouth, then have someone pour the peppermint schnapps down the luge as you catch it in your mouth. It tastes just like a Peppermint Patty! If you want to get fancy and pay a bit more money, they can sculpt the ice into a design of your choice. I've seen glass slippers, a gun, and even human anatomy. A luge is always a big hit at a party!

WWW.
Drinking
Around
TheWorld.com

**BOTTLE OF
RUSSIAN VODKA
BOTTLE OF
CARIBBEAN RUM
BOTTLE OF
ITALIAN AMARETTO
BOTTLE OF
MEXICAN TEQUILA
BOTTLE OF GERMAN
JÄGERMIESTER
TRIPLE GALLON OF HAWAIIAN
PUNCH
STYROFOAM COOLER
BAG OF ICE
STYROFOAM CUPS**

You don't have to book a world cruise or visit Epcot to go drinking around the world! Take all of these international bottles and the Hawaiian mixer on a trip to a Styrofoam cooler. Sail in a bag of ice, then stir it all up, world traveler. Grab a *Condé Nast Traveler* mag, and get ready to take your mind as well as your taste buds on a journey around the world. You are such a cosmopolitan!

Tropical Snowball Slushies

BOTTLE OF MANDARIN-FLAVORED VODKA
BOTTLE OF COCONUT RUM
GALLON OF ORANGE JUICE
GALLON OF PINEAPPLE JUICE
LARGE CONTAINER
ICE-CREAM SCOOP
THREE LITERS OF CHILLED SQUIRT, FRESCA, OR OTHER CITRUS SODA
TALL COOL GLASSES

Of all the punches in this chapter, this is one that I have in my freezer right now as your eyeballs are reading this. It's so yummy and is requested every time my sisters, Carolyn and Charlie, come over. You have to prepare it the day before to have it ready, but it's so easy! Just take a big Tupperware container from your cabinet, and pour in the mandarin-flavored vodka, coconut rum, orange juice, and pineapple juice. Stir it all up, then stick it in the freezer. When it's frozen, scoop out a coupla scoops into a tall cool glass, fill with citrus soda of some sort, and serve with a spoon (Fresca, by the way, has zero calories). Be careful! These Tropical Snowball Slushies are potent, even though they don't taste that way.

133

Born to Be Wild Berry Punch

BOTTLE OF BERRY-
FLAVORED VODKA
BOTTLE OF BLACKBERRY
BRANDY
BOTTLE OF WILD-BERRY
SCHNAPPS
FOUR CUPS OF CRANBERRY JUICE
QUARTER GALLON OF FROZEN
STRAWBERRIES
GALLON OF LEMONADE
COUPLA PINTS OF FRESH STRAWBERRIES
PLASTIC FRUIT-SHAPED CONTAINERS FILLED
WITH CANDY PIXY STIX POWDER
FRESH GRAPES, BANANAS, APPLES, AND
ANY FRUITS IN SEASON
BIG PUNCH BOWL WITH LADLE
WILD GLASSWARE

If you were born to be wild and happen to be looking for adventure for whatever comes your way, then this punch will get your motor running! Begin by blending the frozen strawberries together with the lemonade and candy powder to make the mix. (The plastic fruit-shaped containers of powdered candy can be found in every mall candy store.) Then stick it in the fridge. Next, fill up the empty fruit-shaped containers with H_2O, screw the caps back on, and freeze. When your wild party is about to begin, pour all the ingredients and mixers in a big punch bowl and drop in the frozen plastic fruit to keep it all cool. Garnish the entire rim of the bowl with fresh strawberries (just press the strawberries gently onto the rim). Decorate all around the bowl with the rest of the fresh fruit, and each of your born-to-be-wild friends will feel like a true nature's child after exploring this berry-berry liquid adventure!

● ● ● ● ● ● ● ● ● ● ● ● ● ● ● ● ● ● ●

BOTTLE OF TUACA
BOTTLE OF VANILLA-
FLAVORED VODKA
GALLON OF TEA
GALLON OF APPLE CIDER
ALLSPICE
GINGER
CINNAMON STICK
LARGE PUNCH BOWL WITH LADLE
EXTRA-LARGE BOWL WITH ICE
HALF-GALLON MILK CARTON
TALL ICED-TEA GLASSES

Boston Tea Party Splash

You don't have to dress up like a Mohawk Indian and sneak aboard a ship to splash this tea! Go out and buy all the ingredients you'll need for this party splash, and pay the taxes on it, colonist. To keep everything chilly, set a punch bowl into an extra-large bowl of ice, then throw in the Boston Tea Party Splash. Place some plastic toy ships in, if that floats your boat. I'm sure your guests from up and down the coast will pass this tea act without any resistance!

Wake Up and Smell the Roasted Coffee Buzz

BOTTLE OF COFFEE LIQUEUR
BOTTLE OF IRISH CREAM
TWO POTS OF COLD STRONG
COFFEE
FOUR CUPS OF CREAM
SUGAR TO TASTE
PINT OF CHOCOLATE OR
VANILLA ICE CREAM
SPRINKLE THE CINNAMON
LARGE PUNCH BOWL WITH LADLE
COOL COFFEE CUPS

136

All of your java junkies will agree that you are the Master of the Roast when you serve up this grind! Mix this drip into a big punch bowl, float it with ice cream, sprinkle with cinnamon, and invite your friends over for a little coffee break. Serve up this cup of joe with a doughnut so that your friends can get to dunkin'. To make it all pretty and inviting, decorate with doughnuts all around the bowl, and this buzz will be guaranteed to taste good to the last drop!

Strip-and-Go-Naked Trash Can-Poker Punch

BOTTLE OF VODKA
BOTTLE OF GIN
CASE OF BEER
DOUBLE GALLON OF LIMEADE OR LEMONADE
CLEAN TRASH CAN
NEW, NEVER-USED-FOR-FUEL ONE-GALLON FUEL CAN
DECK OF PLAYING CARDS
PLASTIC GLASSES

This trashy punch sounds like something you might find at a nudist colony, streakers convention, or strip-poker party! Start by filling up an empty and clean gallon fuel can with H_2O then stick it in the freezer. When your potentially nude party is about to begin, pour the raw vodka, gin, beer, and lemonade into the trash can, then drop in the frozen fuel can to keep the punch cold. Scatter a deck of playing cards (nudie-girl cards would make a nice touch) faceup all around the trash can, and let the skinny-dippin' begin!

For an ice-breaker, buy a deck of blue-backed cards for the guys and red-backed cards for the girls, putting the blue cards in a blue box and the red cards in a red box. When your guests arrive, the guys pick a card from the blue box, and the girls pick a card from the red box. The game is to find the other person with your matching card. If your guests are not heterosexual, adjust the boxes as necessary.

DOUBLE BOTTLE OF DARK RUM

DOUBLE JIG THE 151 PROOF RUM

DOUBLE GALLON OF EGGNOG

QUART OF EGGNOG ICE CREAM

SPRINKLE THE CINNAMON

MATCHES

BIG PUNCH BOWL WITH LADLE

FESTIVE WREATH

HOLIDAY CUPS

Grandma's Flaming Tree-Trimming Cheer

If there's anybody who has trimmed trees more than anyone else, it's Grandma! She's not only an expert tree trimmer, she knows how to make the best tree-trimming cheer, so she gave me this recipe to share with you! Grandma says to pour the dark rum and eggnog in a punch bowl that is set into a festive wreath. To keep it cold, float the eggnog ice cream in the cheer. Grandma's favorite part is when she pours the 151 proof rum on top of the ice cream and turns down the lights. She then ignites the 151 proof rum, and as the flames rise, she holds the cinnamon high and sprinkles it on them. It's like a mini indoor holiday firework show. After the flames die down, she flips on the lights and serves up the cheer in cups. Our tree-trimming get-togethers always turn out pretty creative, thanks to Grandma's Flaming Tree-Trimming Cheer!

Hillbilly Idol Lemonade

BOTTLE OF CITRUS-FLAVORED VODKA

DOUBLE BOTTLE OF JACK DANIEL'S

DOUBLE GALLON OF COUNTRY TIME LEMONADE

THREE FRESH LEMONS

COOLER

BAG OF ICE

PLASTIC GLASSES

Just one sip of this rockin' lemonade will have you in the midnight hour yellin', "More, more, more!" Grab a cooler, and rock it with the citrus-flavored vodka, Jack Daniel's, and lemonade, then throw in three sliced lemons and a bag of ice. Stir it up good, give a rebel yell, and get to sippin', rockabilly! If your lemonade stand runs dry, just make more, more, more!

**TWO LARGE CANS OF
FROZEN GRAPE JUICE
TWO LARGE CANS OF
FROZEN
APPLE JUICE
HALF TEASPOON OF DRY
YEAST
EIGHT CUPS OF SUGAR
DOUBLE GALLON OF DISTILLED
WATER
TWO LARGE BOWLS
TWO GLASS GALLON JUGS
TWO THICK TOY PUNCHING BALLOONS
FUNNEL
STRING
LARGE POT
EMPTY STERILIZED WINE BOTTLES OR
OTHER DECANTERS
CHEESE, CRACKERS, AND FRUIT
WINEGLASSES**

Hot-Air
Balloon Wine
and Cheese Party

Your guests will go up, up, and away with this beautiful homemade balloon wine! That's right! You are going to make your own homemade wine. Let the frozen cans of juice thaw, then pour into two separate bowls. In each container add a quarter teaspoon of yeast and four cups of sugar. Funnel one of the bowls into a glass gallon jug. Do the same with the other bowl and gallon jug. Fill both jugs with distilled water all the way up to the necks, and attach a punching balloon to each, securing it well with string. Set the jugs in a quiet place where they will not be disturbed for three weeks. During this time, you will get to watch the balloons inflate like big hot-air balloons. The wine is ready when the balloons deflate all the way back down. When that happens, carefully pour it into a large pot, paying special attention not to disturb the sediment in the bottom of the jugs. Throw the sediment away. You can now transfer your homemade wine into your own empty and sterilized wine bottles or any other decanters that you prefer. I think that bottles with homemade wine labels would be a nice touch. Chill the wine in the fridge and wait for your guests to arrive. Now, start milking your cow, gathering the grain, and wait!—you *could* make your own cheese and crackers, too, but this is not a cookbook, and I'm not Martha Stewart! Just have wineglasses set out with an assortment of store-bought cheese, fruit, and crackers, then maybe decorate with a few balloons to celebrate your first homemade balloon wine party with your winey friends.

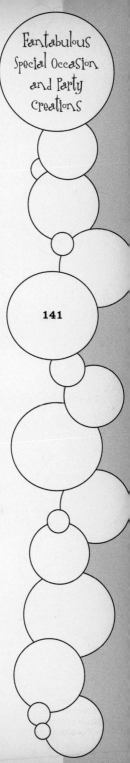

141

BOTTLE OF COCONUT RUM
BOTTLE OF PEACH SCHNAPPS
BOTTLE OF BANANA
LIQUEUR
BOTTLE OF 151 PROOF
RUM
DOUBLE GALLON OF BLUE
KOOL-AID
TWO LITERS OF 7UP
BAG OF ICE
TWENTY FEET OF CLEAR TUBING FROM THE
HARDWARE STORE
FISH TANK

Tropical
Fish Tank
Punch

Here's a fun idea for a college party! Start with a sanitized fish tank, and swim in the coconut rum, peach schnapps, banana liqueur, rum, blue Kool-Aid, ice, and 7UP. Pick up some clear tubing at the hardware store, and cut into straws for the school of fish whom you call friends. Upon entering the party, everyone receives their own big straw to suck out of the community party fish tank. Get to suckin', little fishy! (Maybe for snacks you can serve the little Goldfish crackers.)

Out-of-This-World Cocktails

Potable Destination Cocktails from Around the World

Welcome, thirsty traveler! It has been said that a journey of a thousand drinks begins with one sip, so get ready to go where no man or woman has gone before, and embark on a liquid journey around the globe. On this voyage you will discover destination cocktails that are also out of this world, full of new sights, tastes, and smells. While exploring these potable liquids, please don't be your own guide and drink and drive. Take the guided tour, nomad.

**DOUBLE OUNCE YOUR
FAVORITE WHISKEY
HALF OUNCE THE SWEET
VERMOUTH
DASH A BITTERS
DROP THE MARASCHINO CHERRY
ROCKS GLASS OR MARTINI GLASS**

Manhattan

Start pouring the booze in a shaker today, and wake up like the city that never sleeps. Strain it all into a martini glass like you're the king of the hill, then top off the heap with a drop of a maraschino cherry. Soon you'll feel those little-town blues start melting away. Remember, if you can make it here, you can make it anywhere!

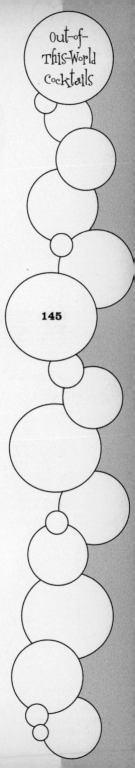

Jamaica Me Crazy

JIG THE DARK RUM
HALF JIG THE TIA MARIA
HALF JIG THE BANANA
LIQUEUR
FILL WITH PINEAPPLE JUICE
GARNISH WITH A MARASCHINO
CHERRY
TALL COOL GLASS

Hey, mon! Got a love for de islands but gotta do de work-a-day ting? No problem! Bring de islands to you. First, put all de ingredients into a tall cool glass of ice, ease into a spiffy tropical shirt, den put a little reggae on de music machine. Ahhh . . . you Jamaica Me Crazy, mon!

145

Sloe Boat to China

PONY THE VODKA
HALF PONY THE SLOE GIN
QUARTER PONY THE
TRIPLE SEC
QUARTER PONY THE FRESH-
SQUEEZED LEMON JUICE
FILL WITH ORANGE JUICE
GARNISH WITH A KUMQUAT
AND ORANGE PEEL
TALL COOL GLASS

Slow down and take a Sloe Boat to China, cruise lover! Sail the vodka, sloe gin, triple sec, and fresh-squeezed lemon juice and orange juice into a tall cool glass of ice, and stir. Garnish with a kumquat and orange peel, stick in a straw, and enjoy the ride.

JIG THE DARK RUM
JIG THE COCONUT RUM
FILL WITH PINEAPPLE JUICE
HALF JIG THE GRENADINE
GARNISH WITH A PINEAPPLE
SLICE AND A MARASCHINO
CHERRY
TALL COOL GLASS

Bahama
Mama

Take a liquid tropical trip to a Caribbean
island! Grab a tall tropical glass of ice
and breeze in the dark rum, coconut rum,
pineapple juice, and grenadine. Garnish that
rim with a cherry-speared pineapple slice,
stick in a straw, and set sail for the islands.

147

Singapore Slingshot

JIG THE GIN
FLOAT A HALF JIG OF
CHERRY BRANDY
JIG THE SWEET-N-SOUR
SPLASHA GRENADINE
SPLASHA SODA WATER
MARASCHINO CHERRY GARNISH
MARTINI GLASS OR SHOOTER GLASS

This Slingshot aims to please! Load up the gin, grenadine, and sweet-n-sour in a shaker tin of ice, then shake and strain into a martini glass. Top it off by splashing the soda water then floating the cherry brandy. This sling is fully loaded now, so shoot it back, hotshot!

148

Long Island Iced Tea (New York Iced Tea)

HALF OUNCE THE VODKA
HALF OUNCE THE GIN
HALF OUNCE THE RUM
HALF OUNCE THE TEQUILA
HALF OUNCE THE
TRIPLE SEC
DOUBLE JIG
THE SWEET-N-SOUR
SPLASHA COLA
LEMON GARNISH
TALL COOL GLASS

149

Here's the most popular concoction to ever come out of Long Island! Start building this tea in a tall cool glass of ice with the vodka, gin, rum, tequila, triple sec, sweet-n-sour, and a splasha cola. Stir it up, stick a lemon on the rim, and your taste buds will hardly believe that this powerful concoction tastes just like tea!

FYI—If you replace the cola with cranberry juice, it's called a Long Beach Iced Tea.

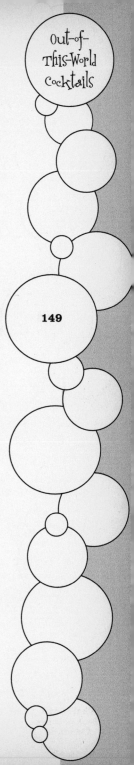

**PONY THE SOUTHERN
COMFORT
PONY THE AMARETTO
PONY THE SLOE GIN
FILL WITH ORANGE JUICE
TALL COOL GLASS**

Alabama
Slammer

This extremely popular libation is the best thing to come out of Alabama! Fill a tall cool glass with the Southern Comfort, amaretto, sloe gin, and orange juice, then stick a straw in and stir. Alabama never tasted so good!

Cuba Libre
with the
captain

**JIG THE CAPTAIN
MORGAN RUM
FILL WITH COLA
GARNISH WITH
LIME WEDGE
HIGHBALL GLASS**

Try this classic with the captain! In a high-ball glass of ice pour in the Captain Morgan Rum, then fill with cola. Garnish with a slice of lime, and now you can have a Cuba Libre *con El Capitán*.

Mississippi Mudslide

PONY THE COFFEE LIQUEUR
PONY THE IRISH CREAM
PONY THE SOUTHERN
COMFORT
FILL WITH CREAM
TALL COOL GLASS

The muddy Mississippi River has a million stories! Start playing in this mud by slippin' a tall cool glass of ice with the coffee liqueur, Irish cream, Southern Comfort, and cream. A couple of these, and you'll be flowing with Mississippi Mudslide stories!

151

PONY THE **151** PROOF RUM
PONY THE RUM
PONY THE BLACKBERRY
BRANDY
PONY THE BANANA LIQUEUR
HALF JIG THE LIME JUICE
HALF JIG THE GRENADINE
GARNISH WITH FANCY FRUIT
TALL COOL GLASS

Florida
Rum Runner

This is the best Rum Runner in the world! Get that blender out, beach baby, and throw in the rums, blackberry brandy, banana liqueur, lime juice, grenadine, and a cupa ice. Push those buttons with your Coppertone fingers, then blend, blend, blend. Pour it into a tall cool glass, garnish it with fancy fruit, and stick in a straw. It represents Florida very well.

HALF PONY THE BRANDY
HALF PONY THE SHERRY
PONY THE TEQUILA ROSE
PONY THE STRAWBERRY-
FLAVORED VODKA
FILL WITH SWEET-N-SOUR
AND CRANBERRY JUICE
STRAWBERRY GARNISH
TEXAS-SIZE TALL COOL GLASS

All My Exes
Live in Texas
Kool-Aid

They say everything in Texas is big, and this drink is no exception. Rustle up a Texas-size glass of ice and pour in all the exes, brandy, sherry, and Tequila Rose. Now add the strawberry vodka, sweet-n-sour, and cranberry juice, and stir it up, good cowboy. Garnish with a summertime strawberry, stick in a big straw, and let your taste buds sample those exes one more time.

Blue Hawaiian Punch

JIG THE **151** PROOF RUM
JIG THE BLUE CURAÇAO
FILL WITH SWEET-N-SOUR
AND PINEAPPLE JUICE
GARNISH
WITH A PINEAPPLE
SLICE AND MARASCHINO CHERRY
TALL COOL GLASS

This Blue Hawaiian has a little punch to it! Pour in the rum, blue curaçao, sweet-n-sour, and pineapple juice. Garnish with a cherry-speared pineapple slice, grab a lei, and do a little hula, baby!

• • • • • • • • • • • • • • • • • •

Spanish Fly

PONY THE VANILLA-FLAVORED
VODKA
PONY THE TEQUILA
FILL WITH COLA
GARNISH WITH A
MARASCHINO
CHERRY
TALL COOL GLASS

If you're looking for a liquid aphrodisiac, then try this little fly. Swat the vanilla-flavored vodka, tequila, and cola in a tall cool glass. Stick in a straw, and drop in the cherry. You'll be in the mood in no time at all.

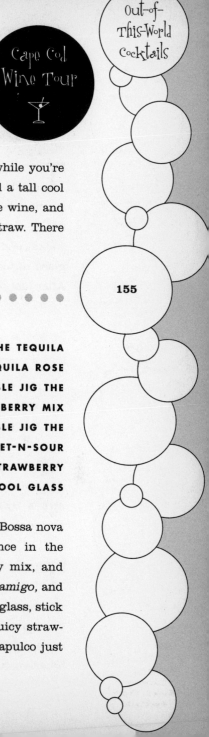
JIG THE VODKA
DOUBLE JIG THE WHITE
WINE
FILL WITH CRANBERRY JUICE
TALL COOL GLASS

Cape Cod Wine Tour

Take a trip to Cape Cod and while you're there, go on a wine tour! Fill a tall cool glass of ice with the vodka, white wine, and cranberry juice, then stick in a straw. There are no sour grapes here!

155

Fun in Acapulco

JIG THE TEQUILA
JIG THE TEQUILA ROSE
DOUBLE JIG THE
STRAWBERRY MIX
DOUBLE JIG THE
SWEET-N-SOUR
GARNISH WITH A STRAWBERRY
TALL COOL GLASS

It's hard to say no to Acapulco! Bossa nova over to the blender, and dance in the tequila, Tequila Rose, strawberry mix, and sweet-n-sour. Push those buttons, *amigo,* and blend it good. Pour into a tall cool glass, stick in a straw, and garnish with a juicy strawberry. It's time to have Fun in Acapulco just like Elvis did!

Greek Goddess of Love

PONY THE OUZO
PONY THE VODKA
PONY THE RASPBERRY
LIQUEUR
HIGHBALL GLASS

This drink is named after Aphrodite, the goddess of love, desire, and beauty. It's meant to be sipped, savored, and enjoyed. Try a taste of this goddess by pouring in the ouzo, vodka, and raspberry liqueur in a highball glass of ice, and sip with a cocktail straw. After just one, you'll be feeling lots of love!

● ● ● ● ● ● ● ● ● ● ● ● ● ● ● ● ● ●

JIG THE CROWN ROYAL
CANADIAN WHISKEY
JIG THE PEACH SCHNAPPS
FILL WITH ORANGE JUICE
AND SWEET-N-SOUR
GARNISH WITH AN ORANGE
AND A MARASCHINO CHERRY
TALL COOL GLASS

Canadian Moose Juice

Try this Canadian Moose Juice, eh? Grab a tall cool glass of ice, eh, and pour in the whiskey, peach schnapps, orange juice, and sweet-n-sour. Garnish it with an orange and cherry, eh, and mix it up with a straw. It won't take long to get loose with this moose juice!

JIG THE COCONUT RUM
JIG THE GOLD TEQUILA
FILL WITH PINEAPPLE JUICE
GARNISH WITH A PINEAPPLE
AND A MARASCHINO CHERRY
KRAZY STRAW GLASSES
TALL COOL GLASS

Sunbathing on a Mexican Beach

Save the airfare to Mexico and just go Sunbathing on a Mexican Beach! Mix up this suntan-lotion potion in a tall cool glass of ice filled with coconut rum, gold tequila, and pineapple juice. Top it off with a juicy slice of pineapple, a cherry, and then put on your clear plastic Krazy Straw glasses. (Krazy Straw glasses can be found in party stores. You know, they're the ones where one end goes in your drink, the liquid goes up the straw, behind your ears, around your eyes, over your nose, and through your lips.) Now that you have your shades on, just be careful to not get sunburned!

Viva Las Vegas

HALF JIG THE SEAGRAM'S 7
HALF JIG THE LICOR 43
HALF JIG THE PIMM'S NO. 1
HALF JIG THE 151 PROOF RUM
FILL WITH 7UP
GARNISH WITH LEMON
TALL COOL GLASS

Are you feeling lucky? Then try playing these numbers, high roller! Lay out a tall glass of ice and throw in the Seagram's 7, Licor 43, Pimm's No. 1, and rum, then fill with 7UP. Garnish with a lemon and stir with a straw. You'll be hitting the jackpot in no time.

● ● ● ● ● ● ● ● ● ● ● ● ● ● ●

Norwegian Mountain Stream

PONY THE VODKA
PONY THE AQUAVIT
PONY THE LIME JUICE
FILL WITH 7UP
HIGHBALL GLASS

Norway is a ruggedly beautiful country of mountains and fjords, and this is one of its most popular cocktails. Grab a highball glass of tiny glaciers and pour in the vodka, Aquavit, lime juice, and 7UP. Now you can experience the land of the midnight sun without leaving home.

Scrumptious Candy Shoppe Cocktails

Delectable Concoctions to Satisfy Any Sweet Tooth

Do you want your cake and want to eat it, too? Then wait until you taste these Scrumptious Candy Shoppe Cocktails. I promise that you'll feel like you are exploring forbidden rooms of the Willy Wonka Chocolate Factory. The next several pages are filled with mouthwatering, good 'n' plenty cocktails to satisfy any sweet tooth. And remember, even though many of these goodies are low in alcohol, be a sweetheart and don't drink and drive, or you'll experience what it's like to take candy away from a baby.

Girl Scout Cookie

DOUBLE PONY THE COFFEE LIQUEUR

JIG THE PEPPERMINT SCHNAPPS

DOUBLE OUNCE THE CREAM

HIGHBALL GLASS OR TALL COOL GLASS

If those yearly Thin Mints make your taste buds jump for joy, then throw all this goodness over a glass of ice, and you won't have to answer the door when the Scouts come knocking. For a summertime treat, try this cookie in the blender!

160

• • • • • • • • • • • • • • • •

PONY THE CHERRY BRANDY

PONY THE VANILLA-FLAVORED VODKA

PONY THE IRISH CREAM

HALF PONY THE GRENADINE

FILL WITH CRANBERRY JUICE

GARNISH WITH A MARASCHINO CHERRY

TALL COOL GLASS

I cannot Tell a Lie Cherry Pie

The story about George Washington and the cherry tree may not be true, but I cannot tell a lie about this cherry-pie libation! It's great! Fill a tall cool glass with ice and stir in all the ingredients. Stick in a straw, drop the cherry, and enjoy, cherry-pie lover!

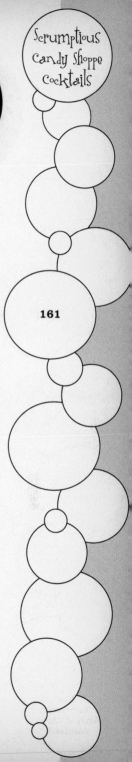

**JIG THE COFFEE LIQUEUR
FILL WITH ORANGE JUICE
HIGHBALL GLASS**

Tootsie Roll Pop

Just how many licks does it take to get to the Tootsie Roll center of a Tootsie Pop? No one knows. But I do know that if you mix these ingredients together, it will only take *one* sip for you to discover that it tastes exactly like a Tootsie Roll Pop. Try it! You'll be pleasantly surprised!

161

● ● ● ● ● ● ● ● ● ● ● ● ● ● ● ● ●

Scooby-Dooby-Doo Snack

**PONY THE
MELON LIQUEUR
PONY THE
COCONUT RUM
FILL WITH
PINEAPPLE JUICE
AND CREAM
TALL COOL GLASS**

Play some groovy background music, then catch a clue and shake all the ingredients in a shaker tin of ice. Pour into a tall cool glass, but don't go jumping into the Mystery Machine after a few of these, because there are ghosts and monsters out there, dude. "Scooby-dooby-doo, where are you?"

Double-Layer Pineapple Upside-Down Cake

PONY THE VODKA
PONY THE IRISH CREAM
PONY THE BUTTERSCOTCH SCHNAPPS
DOUBLE OUNCE THE PINEAPPLE JUICE
GARNISH WITH A MARASCHINO CHERRY
MARTINI GLASS

No ten-step cooking lessons needed for this yummy treat! Grab a shaker, fill it with the giggle juice, and shake it inside, outside, upside down. Strain it all into a martini glass, drop the cherry, and enjoy, sugarcakes!

● ● ● ● ● ● ● ● ● ● ● ● ● ● ●

Frozen Creamsicle

JIG THE BANANA LIQUEUR
JIG THE VANILLA-FLAVORED VODKA
FILL WITH ORANGE JUICE AND CREAM
TALL COOL GLASS

Bring back those childhood memories by throwing all the ingredients in a tall cool glass of ice for measurement's sake. Now pour it all in a blender, and punch those buttons, baby. Pour it all back into the glass, stick in the straw, and slip-slide away to Creamsicle-land.

**JIG THE BLACKBERRY
BRANDY
JIG THE ANISETTE
HIGHBALL GLASS**

Jelly Belly
Bean

Hey, jelly head! Don't wait around for the Easter Bunny to bring you jelly beans! Grab a highball glass, fill it with ice, and jig the ingredients. This Jelly Belly Bean also tastes great straight up as a sipper in a snifter or frozen from a blender.

Shaved-White
Chocolate
Wedding Cake

**PONY THE GODIVA WHITE
CHOCOLATE LIQUEUR
PONY THE AMARETTO
DOUBLE OUNCE THE CREAM
HIGHBALL GLASS**

You don't have to walk down the aisle or fly to Vegas to tie the knot to enjoy this delectable concoction. Forget the blood test, and vow to please yourself by placing all these delectable ingredients in a highball glass of ice. Mmmmmmm . . . wedding cake without all the hassles, and never alimony!

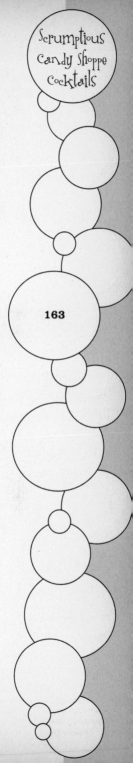

Scrumptious
Candy Shoppe
Cocktails

163

Jolly Rancher

**PONY THE MELON LIQUEUR
PONY THE RASPBERRY
LIQUEUR
PONY THE VODKA
FILL WITH
CRANBERRY JUICE
AND SWEET-N-SOUR
JOLLY RANCHERS
(FLAVOR OF CHOICE)
TALL COOL GLASS**

Jolly Ranchers probably hold the record for causing the most damage to adult teeth, but no worries with this Jolly Rancher, big boy! Pour it all in a tall cool glass, then bite and suck as hard as you want. You're all grown up now, right?

JIG THE VODKA

HALF JIG THE BLUE

CURAÇAO

HALF JIG THE BANANA

LIQUEUR

HALF JIG THE AMARETTO

FILL WITH SWEET-N-SOUR AND

CRANBERRY JUICE

FLOAT VALENTINE HEARTS ON TOP

TALL COOL GLASS

Sweetheart
Sweet Tart

Looking for an aphrodisiac to share with your sweetheart on Valentine's Day? Well, this is it! Lovingly pour all the sweetness into a tall cool glass of ice. Stir, then float the Valentine candy hearts on top. Kiss me, hug me, drink me, baby.

165

Rooty-Tooty Root Beer Float

JIG THE VANILLA-FLAVORED VODKA
JIG THE GALLIANO
JIG THE CREAM
FILL WITH COLA
TOP WITH WHIPPED CREAM
TALL COOL GLASS

You are not going to believe your taste buds with this tasty treat! As unbelievable as this recipe sounds, it really does taste exactly like a Root Beer Float. Mix it all up, top with the whipped cream, then stick a straw in, and suck it down. I promise you'll be pleasantly surprised!

● ● ● ● ● ● ● ● ● ● ● ● ● ● ● ●

Frozen Almond Joy Candy Bar

PONY THE COCONUT RUM
PONY THE AMARETTO
PONY THE DARK CRÈME DE CACAO
FILL WITH CREAM
TALL COOL GLASS

Sometimes you feel like a nut and just want your candy from the freezer! Take a five-minute vacation, and fill a tall cool glass of ice with all these goodies, then throw it all in a blender. Pour it back into the tall cool glass, and enjoy. If you don't feel like a nut and want a Mounds Candy Bar instead, just leave out the amaretto, because sometimes you feel like a nut, and sometimes you don't!

● ● ● ● ● ● ● ● ● ● ● ● ● ● ● ● ●

PONY THE RUM
PONY THE BANANA LIQUEUR
PONY THE PEACH SCHNAPPS
FILL WITH ORANGE JUICE
SPLASHA GRENADINE
HIGHBALL GLASS

Double-Bubble Gum

The only bubble you'll be able to blow with this bubble gum is through your straw! Grab a highball glass and add all the ingredients, then stir it by blowing through your straw. This is one piece of gum that won't lose its flavor or stick to the bedpost!

Oatmeal Cookie with Raisins

PONY THE IRISH CREAM
PONY THE GOLDSCHLAGER
PONY THE JÄGERMEISTER
FILL WITH CREAM
HIGHBALL GLASS

If you can't make it to Grandma's house, then make your own Oatmeal Cookie with Raisins! Mix up the Irish cream, Goldschlager, Jägermeister, and cream in a highball glass, then sit back and enjoy, cookie monster.

● ● ● ● ● ● ● ● ● ● ● ● ● ● ● ● ● ● ●

PONY THE COCONUT RUM
PONY THE DARK CRÈME
DE CACAO
PONY THE FRANGELICO
FILL WITH CREAM
HIGHBALL GLASS

German Chocolate Cake

How does the saying go? "If I knew you were coming, I would've baked a cake"? Well, forget the oven mitts, dude, and just liquefy this home-warming cake for your guests! Mix everything up in a glass of ice, and you'll be good to go, chocolate lover.

HALF JIG THE CINNAMON SCHNAPPS

HALF JIG THE BUTTERSCOTCH SCHNAPPS

HALF JIG THE FRANGELICO

HALF JIG THE IRISH CREAM

FILL WITH CREAM

TOP WITH WHIPPED CREAM

SPRINKLE THE CINNAMON

TALL COOL GLASS

Cinnamon Roll with Frosting

They say that fresh-baked cinnamon rolls are a male's number-one favorite scent. Well, ladies, capture his taste buds with this seductive concoction as well. Mix everything up in a tall cool glass, but fair warning—you and your man might not make it out of the kitchen!

169

PONY THE BANANA LIQUEUR
PONY THE COFFEE LIQUEUR
PONY THE TEQUILA ROSE
CUPA ICE
FILL WITH MILK
TOP WITH WHIPPED CREAM
PUT A MARASCHINO CHERRY ON TOP,
PRETTY PLEASE
TALL COOL GLASS

Banana-
Split Shake

You're never too old for a Banana Split, so try this grown-up version by throwing all the ingredients in a blender with a cup of ice. Pour into a tall cool glass, top with whipped cream, and don't forget the cherry. You can straw your creation or just grab a spoon and dig in lickety-split!

Mint-Chocolate Chip Ice Cream

JIG THE VODKA
HALF JIG THE WHITE CRÈME DE CACAO
HALF JIG THE PEPPERMINT SCHNAPPS
HALF JIG THE IRISH CREAM
HALF JIG THE COFFEE LIQUEUR
FILL WITH CREAM
TALL COOL GLASS

Make your own ice cream! Rock salt is not required. Pour the ingredients into a tall cool glass, then throw it all into a blender. Push some buttons and whirl it around, then soon you'll be enjoying your very own homemade adult ice cream. You're so handy around the house!

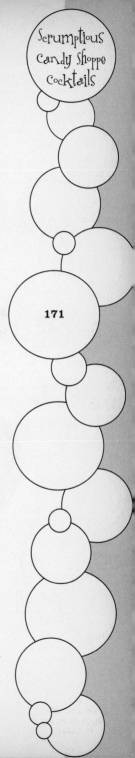

171

HALF JIG THE VODKA
HALF JIG THE AMARETTO
HALF JIG THE CRÈME DE CACAO
THREE PEANUTS
MARTINI GLASS

Baby Ruth Bar

Even the snobs at the country club in the movie *Caddyshack* would love this Baby Ruth Bar! Drop three peanuts into a martini glass, then shake the vodka, amaretto, and crème de cacao in a shaker tin of ice. Strain it all into the glass, and you'll soon realize that being a member of the club never tasted so good.

● ● ● ● ● ● ● ● ● ● ● ● ● ● ● ● ●

Cream Soda Snow Cone

JIG THE VANILLA-FLAVORED VODKA
FILL WITH GINGER ALE
CRUSHED ICE
TALL COOL GLASS

You will barely believe your taste buds as you devour this snow cone! Try one of Miss Charming's favorite recipes by filling a tall cool glass with crushed ice, vanilla-flavored vodka, and ginger ale. Stick in a straw/spoon, and enjoy! Mmmmmm, it tastes exactly like cream soda!

Sultry After-Dinner Drinks

Toddies Guaranteed to Warm Up Any Cold Heart

Need a voyage in a cup when it's coffee, tea, or me time? Then try these flavor-packed, full-bodied, intense aroma–lingering Sultry After-Dinner Drinks that are guaranteed to comfort and leave a lasting impression. Remember, these liquids are good to the last buzzed drop, so don't get captured in the essence of it all by drinking and driving in your cute little mocha barista britches.

**PONY THE CHERRY BRANDY
PONY THE COFFEE LIQUEUR
FILL WITH HOT COCOA
TOP WITH MARSHMALLOWS
COFFEE MUG**

**Enchanted
Black Cherry
Forest Cocoa**

Once upon a time long, long ago, there was an enchanted black cherry forest. It was filled with cherry brandy, coffee liqueur and hot chocolate. One day, marshmallows fell from the sky and landed right on top of the forest. Everyone in the village enjoyed the black cherry forest with marshmallows on top very much, and they lived happily ever after.

● ● ● ● ● ● ● ● ● ● ● ● ● ● ● ● ●

**Cinnamon
Toast with
the Captain**

**JIG THE CAPTAIN
MORGAN SPICED RUM
FILL WITH HOT APPLE CIDER
HONEY, SUGAR, AND
CINNAMON FOR RIMMING
CUP OR MUG**

If you've ever been on a cruise (a real cruise, not one of those three-to-four-day ones), you know that not everyone gets to dine with the captain. Well, hold on to the starboard side of your chair, mate, because now you can dine with the captain any night of the week! Just grab a cup and dip the rim into some honey,

honey, then dip again into the cinnamon and sugar. Now pour in the Captain Morgan Spiced Rum and hot apple cider and you're ready to sail with the captain!

● ● ● ● ● ● ● ● ● ● ● ● ● ● ● ● ● ●

A Steamy Ménage à Trois with Sherry, Maria, and Brandy

HALF JIG THE SHERRY
HALF JIG THE
TIA MARIA
HALF JIG THE BRANDY
FILL WITH
STEAMING COFFEE
TOP WITH LOTS OF
WHIPPED CREAM, AND DON'T
FORGET THE CHERRY
COFFEE MUG

Your dreams aren't the only place you can have A Steamy Ménage à Trois with Sherry, Maria, and Brandy. Pour the sherry, Tia Maria, and brandy into a coffee mug, then add the hot steaming coffee to all of them at the same time. Top it all off with whipped cream on top, and don't forget the cherry. Don't ever forget the cherry!

PONY THE COGNAC
PONY THE AMARETTO
SNIFTER

Sonata

One taste of this luxurious sipper and you'll feel like a Sonata is playing on your tongue. In a snifter add the cognac and the amaretto. The cognac is very strong and the amaretto very sweet, so the combination of the two blend together in perfect harmony.

● ● ● ● ● ● ● ● ● ● ● ● ● ● ● ● ● ●

Green Candy Apple Pie à la Mode

JIG THE TUACA
HOT APPLE CIDER
TOP WITH WHIPPED CREAM
GREEN CANDY APPLE
SPOON (RECIPE FOLLOWS)
COFFEE MUG

This flavor-packed toddy will have your taste buds jumping for joy! In a coffee mug add the Tuaca and hot apple cider, then top it with whipped cream and serve with a green candy apple spoon. Do you think this apple a day would keep the doctor away?

Green Candy Apple Spoons

**FOUR CRUSHED
GREEN-APPLE
JOLLY RANCHERS
SPOONA CORN SYRUP
HEAVYWEIGHT PLASTIC
SPOONS
VEGETABLE COOKING SPRAY
WAXED PAPER
SAUCEPAN
JELLY-ROLL PAN**

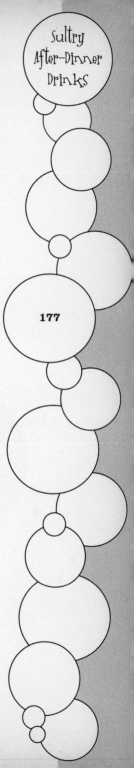

Line a jelly-roll pan with waxed paper, then spray with cooking spray. In a small heavy saucepan, combine the crushed candy and corn syrup over low heat, stirring frequently until the candy melts. Simply spoon melted-candy mixture into the bowl of each plastic spoon, and place the spoons on the waxed paper with the handles on the rim of the pan so that it keeps the spoons level. Let them harden, then you can store them in a plastic bag until you need them. I bet Eve would've loved these!

PONY THE IRISH CREAM
PONY THE FRANGELICO
FILL WITH HOT COFFEE
TOP WITH WHIPPED CREAM
COFFEE MUG

Hot Nutty Irishman

This smoldering classic is always popular! In a coffee mug add the Irish cream, Frangelico, and hot coffee, then top with whipped cream. Curl up on the couch with a good book, and escape with a Hot Nutty Irishman.

178

● ● ● ● ● ● ● ● ● ● ● ● ● ● ● ● ● ● ● ●

Girls Just Wanna Have Fun With Hot Buttered Rum

BOTTLE OF RUM
HALF A POUND OF "FOR
REAL" BUTTER
POUND OF DARK
BROWN SUGAR
HALF A
GALLON OF VANILLA
ICE CREAM
HOT H$_2$O
ICE-CUBE TRAYS
COFFEE MUGS

Hey, girls! Here's a fun thing to make and save to share with your friends on a cold, chilly night. In a saucepan over low heat, throw in half a pound of "for real" butter and a pound of dark brown sugar. When it's mixed and melted, slowly add the half gallon of vanilla ice cream, stirring it all up well. Take it off the heat and pour it into ice-cube trays, then freeze. When you want a Hot Buttered Rum, just plop a cube in a coffee mug, then add the rum and hot H_2O. For extra fun you can steep a flavored vanilla-maple tea bag in the hot H_2O or use a dark or spiced rum because Girls Just Wanna Have Fun with Hot Buttered Rum! (Makes around 25 servings.)

● ● ● ● ● ● ● ● ● ● ● ● ● ● ● ● ●

Fresh-Baked Georgia Peach Pie

JIG THE PEACH SCHNAPPS
HALF JIG THE IRISH CREAM
PEACH TEA BAG
FILL WITH HOT H_2O
SCOOP OF VANILLA
ICE CREAM
COFFEE MUG

This after-dinner toddy is just peachy! Grab a coffee mug and steep a peach tea bag in the hot H_2O for one minute, then add the peach schnapps, Irish cream, and scoop of vanilla ice cream. You're gonna love a slice of this pie!

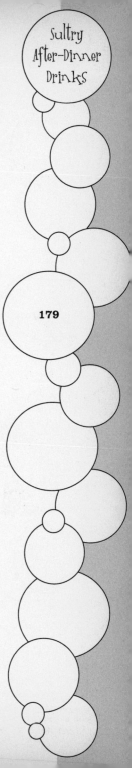

JIG THE VANILLA-FLAVORED
VODKA

HALF JIG THE PEPPERMINT
SCHNAPPS

HALF A CUPA FRESH SLICED
GINGER

HALF A CUPA FRESH CRANBERRIES

HALF A CUPA CRANBERRY JUICE

DOUBLE CUPA BOILING H$_2$O

PINCH OF NUTMEG

SPOONA HONEY

SPOONA CINNAMON

SPOONA POWDERED SUGAR

TOP WITH WHIPPED CREAM, CANDY
SPRINKLES, AND TWO LICORICE TWIZZLER
STICKS

MEDIUM BOWL

TWO SAUCERS

SAUCEPAN

TWO COFFEE MUGS

Gingerbread
House in a Cup
for Two

This is Hansel and Gretel's favorite! Before you do anything, bring the H$_2$O to a roaring boil and pour it into a bowl filled with the fresh sliced ginger and fresh cranberries, then cover and let stand for twenty minutes. While waiting, pour honey onto one of the saucers. Then spoon the cinnamon and powdered sugar onto the other saucer, mixing them up. Now lightly dip the rims of the two mugs into the honey first, then the cinnamon/sugar mixture and set aside. When the

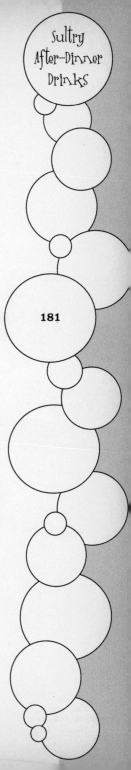

twenty minutes are up, strain the ginger/cranberry liquid back into the saucepan to heat, adding the vanilla-flavored vodka, peppermint schnapps, cranberry juice, and nutmeg while stirring. (Just get it warm enough to drink, don't boil it.) Start building your gingerbread house by pouring the liquid into the cups, then topping with the whipped cream. Sprinkle with candy sprinkles and stick in a licorice stick. (If you bite both ends of the licorce stick off, it can be used as a candy straw.) Boy, Hansel and Gretel really know how to party!

181

● ● ● ● ● ● ● ● ● ● ● ● ● ● ● ● ●

Butter Me Up, Scotty

JIG THE BUTTERSCOTCH SCHNAPPS
HALF JIG THE IRISH CREAM
FILL WITH HOT CHOCOLATE
TOP WITH WHIPPED CREAM AND BUTTERSCOTCH CHIPS
COFFEE MUG

Scotty sure is a pretty talented chief engineer; he knows how to beam *and* butter you up! Grab a coffee mug and add the butterscotch schnapps, Irish cream, and hot chocolate. Top everything off with whipped cream and butterscotch chips. Mmmmm . . . I guess Scotty has been moonlighting in the lounge!

**HALF JIG THE COFFEE
LIQUEUR
HALF JIG THE
IRISH CREAM
HALF JIG THE AMARETTO
FILL WITH HOT COFFEE
TOP WITH WHIPPED CREAM
AND A CHOCOLATE SPOON
(RECIPE FOLLOWS)
COFFEE MUG**

A
Roasted Toast
to the Hostess with
the Mostest

You will be the toast of the town with this Roasted Toast to the Hostess with the Mostest! Pour the coffee liqueur, Irish cream, amaretto, and hot coffee into a coffee mug, then top it off with whipped cream and a chocolate spoon. This mild and mellow brown-liquid goodness is guaranteed to leave your guests with a lasting impression!

**HALFA CUPA SEMISWEET
CHOCOLATE PIECES
SMALL TUBE OF
WHITE ICING
COOKIE SHEET
WAXED PAPER
SAUCEPAN
PLASTIC SPOONS
PLASTIC WRAP**

Place a piece of waxed paper on a cookie sheet large enough to hold about twenty spoons. Next, melt semisweet chocolate pieces in a heavy saucepan over low heat while stirring constantly. Remove from heat and stir until smooth, then dip the spoons into the chocolate, tapping the handle of the spoon against the side of the pan to remove the excess chocolate. Place the spoons on the waxed paper and refrigerate for thirty minutes (or until chocolate is set). With the little white-icing tube decorate the chocolate spoons by making small dots, zigzag lines, circles, hearts, names, initials, sayings, etc. Wrap each spoon separately in clear or colored plastic wrap, and refrigerate them until needed. Cute, huh?

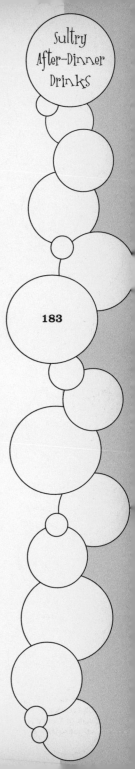

CHILLED BOTTLE
OF HALF
COCONUT RUM
AND HALF
MELON LIQUEUR

BOTTLE OF
ONE-THIRD GIN,
ONE-THIRD
VODKA, AND ONE-
THIRD DRY VERMOUTH

BOTTLE OF VANILLA-
FLAVORED VODKA

WATERMELON

GALLON JAR OF BIG GREEN OLIVES

GALLON JAR OF MARASCHINO CHERRIES

TWO LITERS OF GINGER ALE

BUNCH OF SEASONAL FRUIT

TWO LARGE BOWLS

TWO MEDIUM BOWLS

DUCT TAPE

THREE THICK COTTON TOWELS

ICE

SHAKER TIN

COCKTAIL PICKS

TALL COOL GLASSES

MARTINI GLASSES

Cherry Vanilla-Bomb Ginger Ale, Drunken Olive Martinis, and Spiked Coconut Watermelon

G et ready to impress your guests with a fruity spread that they've probably never seen before! For the Cherry Bombs, pour 90 percent of the juice out of the cherry jar, then fill with the vanilla-flavored vodka.

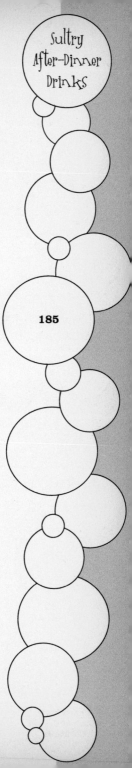

For the Drunken Olives, pour out all the juice from the olive jar and fill with gin, vodka, and dry vermouth, then let both jars sit in the fridge overnight. (To save some dough, try buying the gallon jars of olives and cherries at a bulk store.)

Next, you're going to make two ice bowls to be used as displays for the cherries and olives. Simply take a large bowl and fill it half with water. Put a medium-size bowl into it, weight it down to where the water rises up to the rim, then place it into the freezer. Repeat the process with the other pair of bowls.

Now, for the Coconut Watermelon. First, start with the watermelon prechilled, and clear out enough headroom space in the fridge where the watermelon can sit with a bottle sticking in it. Cut out a hole in the top of the watermelon large enough for the neck of a bottle to fit. Put a prechilled bottle mixture of half coconut rum and half melon liqueur upside down in the hole and duct-tape it securely. Let it sit in the fridge overnight.

Right before your guests arrive, lay out the three thick towels on top of one another, then take out the ice bowls and run a little warm water on them to loosen the bowls from the ice. Next, set the ice bowls on the towels (as they melt, the towels will absorb the water). Take the Cherry Bombs and Drunken Olives out of the fridge and pour into the ice bowls, then place some cocktail picks near the ice bowls.

Are you ready for the Coconut Watermelon? Take out the watermelon, remove the duct tape, and shove the bottle in as deep as you can so that it stays up by itself. This makes for a really cool presentation when your guests arrive. Cover the unattractive towels with a bunch of seasonal fruits like bananas, grapes, apples, etc. You can cut up the watermelon into pieces when the time is right to serve to your guests (I'm sure they'll let you know). Have a shaker tin and martini glasses nearby to make some martinis with the Drunken Olives, and pour ginger ale into some tall cool glasses of ice for the Cherry Bombs. Like I said before, it'll be an impressive spread that your guests have never seen before!

JIGGER THE APRICOT BRANDY
HALF JIG THE COINTREAU
FILL WITH CHILLED
ORANGE JUICE
SCOOP OF VANILLA ICE CREAM
COFFEE CUP OR TALL COOL GLASS

Midsummer
Night's Dream

L ove looks not with the eyes, but with the
mind; and therefore is winged Cupid
painted blind. Start intertwining this
Midsummer Night's Dream by pouring the
apricot brandy, Cointreau, and chilled orange
juice into a cup or a tall cool glass. Top with a
scoop of vanilla ice cream because Shakes-
peare says that love makes fools of us all.

187

JIG THE IRISH CREAM

JIG THE GODIVA
WHITE CHOCOLATE
LIQUEUR

JIG THE AMARETTO

TWO CUPS OF
HALF-AND-HALF,
DIVIDED

HALF A CUPA WHITE CHOCOLATE CHIPS

PINCH OF NUTMEG

SPOONA VANILLA EXTRACT

SAUCEPAN

GLASS MUGS

This Snow White Hot Chocolate is the seven dwarfs' very favorite because it has seven ingredients. Get working on it by singing, "Hi-ho, hi-ho, it's off to work I go. . . ." Grab a saucepan and melt the white chocolate chips, then while stirring, add a quarter cupa the half-and-half and a pinch of nutmeg over low heat. When the chocolate is melted, add the remaining half-and-half and keep stirring until heated. Now remove it from the heat, and add the vanilla extract, Irish cream, Godiva White Chocolate Liqueur, amaretto, then stir again. Pour it into an upright "glass coffin" (glass mug), and remember not to accept any apples from anyone today, because you are the fairest of them all!

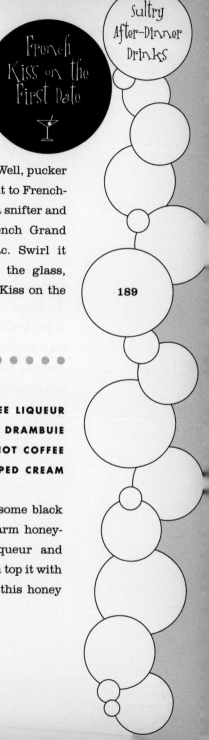

PONY THE GRAND MARNIER
PONY THE COGNAC
SNIFTER

French
Kiss on the
First Date

Do you kiss on the first date? Well, pucker up, *chéri,* because you'll want to French-kiss this sultry sipper! Reach for a snifter and pour in equal parts of the French Grand Marnier and the French cognac. Swirl it around, then put those lips on the glass, because you are about to French Kiss on the First Date. *C'est si bon!*

• • • • • • • • • • • • • • • • • • •

Warm
Black Honey

PONY THE COFFEE LIQUEUR
HALF PONY THE DRAMBUIE
FILL WITH HOT COFFEE
TOP WITH WHIPPED CREAM

Get busy as a bee and make some black honey. Start making this warm honey-comb by pouring the coffee liqueur and Drambuie into the black coffee then top it with whipped cream. Beeeeeee careful, this honey has a sting!

Pyromaniac Lovers Rum

CUPA DARK RUM

JIG THE GRAND MARNIER

BUNCH OF WHOLE CLOVES

TWO THIN-
SKINNED ORANGES

HALF A GALLON OF
APPLE CIDER

CINNAMON STICK

BAKING DISH

LARGE SAUCEPAN (SEE NOTE BELOW)

CUPS

Here's a great recipe from my friends Paco and Erica. There's enough in the recipe to serve ten people, so it's perfect for a pyromaniac holiday get-together! First, grab the oranges and stick a bunch of cloves in them, put them in a baking dish, and bake them for forty-five minutes at 350 degrees. When they are just about done, start heating the cider and cinnamon stick in the large saucepan, then add the baked cloved oranges and prick them with a fork. Now take the saucepan away from the heat and set it somewhere away from all things flammable, but keep visible to all for a fire show (see Note below). Pour the Grand Marnier on the oranges, then light. When the flames die down, add the dark rum, and serve it up, flame lover!

Note: As with any process that involves flames, proper precautions should always be followed. It is recommended that you have a fire extinguisher handy, and that this never be performed alone. Always practice the technique when someone is near.

The saucepan should not be made of nonstick material, or you will burn it. You can also pour the mixture into a chafing dish, disposable aluminum roast pan, or something that won't burn the coating off. If you go to a party store, they have inexpensive aluminum pans with simple metal frames that hold a sterno. A sterno is a can of fuel that you light.

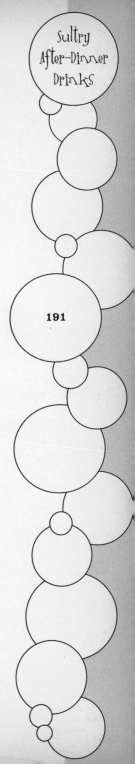

JIG THE DARK RUM

CUPA HOT COCOA

JIG THE CREAM OF

COCONUT

CUPA FLAKED COCONUT

PINT OF VANILLA ICE CREAM

COOKIE SHEET LINED WITH WAXED PAPER

COFFEE MUG

Coconut
Snowball Cocoa

Go cuckoo with coconut cocoa! First, wash your hands, then make tangerine-size ice-cream balls (if it feels too cold and icky to you, use rubber gloves). Immediately roll the balls in the flaked coconut, then place them on a waxed paper–lined cookie sheet and stick them in the freezer. When frozen, you can store them in a freezer bag until you are ready to use them. Make Coconut Snowball Cocoa by grabbing a coffee mug and pouring in the dark rum, hot cocoa, and cream of coconut, then floating a coconut ice-cream ball on top. It may sound cuckoo, but you'll go crazy over this drink, coconut head!

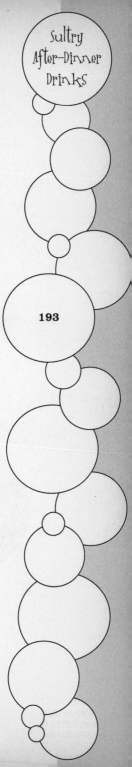

Red-Hot
Vanilla-
Cinnamon Cider

PONY THE CINNAMON
SCHNAPPS
HALF PONY THE VANILLA-
FLAVORED VODKA
FILL WITH
HOT APPLE CIDER
HANDFUL OF CANDY
CINNAMON RED HOTS
COFFEE MUG

This cider is almost too hot to handle! In a coffee mug add the cinnamon schnapps, vanilla-flavored vodka, and hot apple cider. Then reach your hot little hand over and grab a handful of candy Red Hots and drop them in. You're such a hottie tottie!

193

**PONY THE RASPBERRY
LIQUEUR
HALF PONY THE COFFEE
LIQUEUR
FILL WITH HOT
CHOCOLATE AND COFFEE
TOP WITH WHIPPED CREAM
COFFEE MUG**

Berry Good
Hot Chocolate
Go-Go

This Go-Go juice contains no dancers but it is berry good! Just pick up some raspberry liqueur at the store and put it in your basket. At home, pick a coffee mug and pour in the raspberry liqueur and coffee liqueur, then pour in equal amounts of hot chocolate and Go-Go juice (coffee). Add whipped cream on top, and get ready to enjoy this berry good toddy!

Café Diable
(Ka-fay
Dee-a-blay)

**ONE AND A HALF CUPS OF
BRANDY
ONE WHOLE ORANGE
DOUBLE SPOONA SUGAR
DOUBLE CUPA BLACK COFFEE
FOUR WHOLE CLOVES
CHAFING DISH
LADLE
COFFEE MUGS**

After throwing an incredible dinner party, impress your friends even further by making Café Diable for them. Start by peeling the whole orange so that the peel comes off in one long spiral, then set aside. Next, place the brandy, cloves, and sugar into the chafing dish, and heat slowly. Grasp the orange peel by one end (in your left hand if you are right-handed), and hold it above the chafing dish just high enough so that the other end of the peel touches the brandy. Scoop up some brandy with the ladle (with the other hand), then light it from the flame below the chafing dish. Pour the now flaming brandy gently down the orange peel as close to the top as possible. (Be careful not to let any of the flaming brandy splash about; see Note below.) Repeat this process several times then carefully set the orange peel aside onto a non-flammable surface. At this point, you're just about done with your host/hostess with the mostest performance, so all you have to do now is slowly pour the coffee into the chafing dish to extinguish the flames, then serve the Café Diable.

(Note: As with any process that involves flames, proper precautions should always be followed. It is recommended that you have a fire extinguisher handy, and that this never be performed alone. Always practice the technique when someone is near. You can use the same setup described for Pyromaniac Lovers Rum, pages 190–191.)

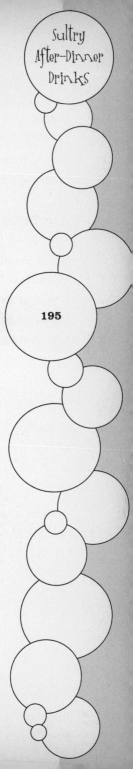

Acknowledgments

Special thanks to my cyber cocktail connoisseur friends for their contributions and support.

John Catlin (www.thebartend.com)

Dale "King Cocktail" Degroff (www.KingCocktail.com)

Kathy Hamlin (www.Cocktails.About.com)

Mark Hastings (www.BarProducts.com)

Robert Hess (www.DrinkBoy.com)

Pål Løberg (www.Webtender.com)

Scott Young (www.ExtremeBartending.com)

Looking for a Recipe?

202

Contact Miss Charming? You Bet!

What's wrong? Not enough recipes to quench your thirst? Then ride those cool electronic waves and surf on over to www.miss-charming.com (no lifeguard on duty).

Need a little more information on a recipe in this book? Maybe you have a question or comment? Or could it be that you need Miss Charming to be the cocktail consultant for *Sex and the City*? She can be reached at cheryl@miss-charming.com.

About the Author

Cheryl Charming has spent more than 20 years entertaining people around the world with her bartending skills (and her black book of crazy cocktails—a much-coveted item wherever she works). Cheryl formerly taught a mandatory bartending class at Walt Disney World. She lives in Florida.

Amaze your friends! Entertain strangers! Win a free beer!

Have fun while wowing those around you with your creativity and dexterity at the bar! Learn to perform eighty tricks using matches, toothpicks, glasses, coins, bottles, napkins, and other items readily available at any party or pub.

- Light a cigar by swiping it across a one-dollar bill
- Pick up a bottle using only a straw
- Make a cup float in the air
- Get a shot of liquor out of an empty bottle

Become the life of the party with Miss Charming's previous book:

MiSS Charming's Book of Bar Amusements: 80 Tricks Guaranteed to Entertain Your Friends, Break the Ice at a Bar, and Liven Up Your Next Party!

by Cheryl Charming

0-609-80508-8

$12.00 paperback (Canada: $17.95)

THREE RIVERS PRESS
Wherever books are sold
www.randomhouse.com